i

The Webster Smith Court-martial,

Justice Is Dead

Unrestricted Coast Guard Chronicles

Volume 02 Number 03

UCGC Vol. 02 Nr 03

DEDICATION

I dedicate this book to my God-parents, CWO Oliver T. Henry, USCG (Ret.) and his loving wife, Jean.

Chief Warrant Officer Oliver T. Henry, USCG, "who through his relentless pursuit to serve the Coast Guard as a skilled petty officer on board the CGC *Northland* during World War Two, successfully moved from the wardroom as a steward to the engine-room as a motor-machinist's mate." [Quoted from "A Call to Serve", a pamphlet published for the U.S. Coast Guard's Anniversary Worship Service on 8 August 1999]. CWO Henry was one of the first African-Americans in the Coast Guard to successfully transfer to a line rating from that of stewardsmate and did so well before the full integration of the Armed Forces.

TABLE OF CONTENTS

NO ENEMIES

YOU HAVE NO ENEMIES, YOU SAY?
ALAS, MY FRIEND, THE BOAST IS POOR.
HE WHO HAS MINGLED IN THE FRAY
OF DUTY, THAT THE BRAVE ENDURE,
MUST HAVE MADE FOES. IF YOU HAVE NONE,
SMALL IS THE WORK THAT YOU HAVE DONE.
YOU'VE HIT NO TRAITOR ON THE HIP,
YOU'VE DASHED NO CUP FROM PERJURED LIP,
YOU'VE NEVER TURNED THE WRONG TO RIGHT,
YOU'VE BEEN A COWARD IN THE FIGHT.
(CHARLES MACKAY)

PREFACE

This is intended to be the definitive word on the first and only court-martial of a United States Coast Guard Academy cadet. The Case of Cadet Webster Smith, The Last Word, UCGC Vol. 02, Nr. 01, was written from the perspective of the accused, Cadet First Class Webster Smith. It was not written from the perspective of his accusers. A prior account of this case focused on the women involved. Conduct Unbecoming an Officer and a Lady told the story of the court-martial from the perspective of the witnesses for the prosecution.

Why this new edition, UCGC Vol. 02 , Nr. 02? There are several reasons. This Case is unique in that this has never happened before. No other Coast Guard Academy Cadet has been punished at a General Court-martial. That is remarkable for a revered institution that has existed 1876.

Also, as is sometimes the case, new evidence has come to light. New witnesses have surfaced that shed more light on this case. This case was more orchestrated by senior officers than first perceived. This was not a court-martial. This was a legal lynching. The perpetrators have been rewarded. The Trial Judge, CAPT Brian Judge, and the Academy Legal Advisor, CDR Sean Gill, have both been promoted to seats on the Coast Guard Court of Criminal appeals.

Moreover, it has been ten years since the trial and conviction. An entire decade has passed. The jail sentence has been served. The Supreme Court Petition for A Writ of Certiorari has been denied. The Clemency Petition was denied. The Record is complete.

Cadet Smith was a senior when the trial began. He was within months of graduating from the Academy, but he was expelled. His career was ruined. His life was irreparably harmed. For ten years he was required to register in the State of Texas as a Sexual offender. He married, had children, and for ten years he was not allowed to attend the birthday parties of his children.

This case has been hotly debated in certain quarters. The Coast Guard has tried its best to forget that this court-martial ever occurred. However, I fear that this case will be debated and talked about for years to come. Long after the political and social climates that gave rise to this Case have abated; cadets, officers, politicians and parents will be discussing the Webster Smith Case.

What distinguishes this book from other books on the case is that this book distinguishes how the Coast Guard Legal Officers and the senior Academy officers disposed of this case as opposed to other cases with similar fact patterns. It contains facts and statements not presented as evidence at the Trial. Here are the witnesses own words contradicting their testimony in court. Emails from the principal prosecuting witness sent to Webster Smith and his mother contemporaneous with the trial are enclosed as Appendix 9.

This Case will serve as a witness to an era in the United States Military and its Service Academies that was ripe with cultural and ethical upheavals, proceedings with plenty of due process and little justice, sexual assaults in the military, retaliation against whistleblowers, mind blowing results, aggravation and frustration.

There were winners and losers. Yes, there was suffering and heart break. The Coast Guard Academy lost. Its integrity was tarnished. Some of its senior officers acted dishonorably. Honor is the moral glue that binds today's officers to the Long Blue Line of former officers.

Contrary to conventional wisdom, this story has a happy ending. Someone once said that you have to break some eggs to make an omelette. Quite a few eggs were broken in this tragedy.

Webster Smith was irreparably harmed. His reputation was damaged. The marriage of his parents was destroyed. His younger brother was not admitted into a Coast Guard Academy preparatory program for which he was considered a certainty.

Through it all Webster Smith was able to maintain a positive attitude. Because of his faith and a few dedicated friends, he emerged from all of his troubles as a happily married man, a father, and a business man.

He graduated with honors with a degree in General Business and Decision Information Science from the University of St. Thomas. He completed two semesters of Russian Linguistics at neighboring Rice University and completed all requirements for the pre-law designation.

Yes, there were winners and there were losers. But Webster Smith was one of the winners. This is his story. It is also the story of Lindsey Deason, his loyal, devoted, and committed wife and the mother of his children.

This American tragedy has a fairy tale ending.

GENERAL COURT-MARTIAL
UNITED STATES COAST GUARD
UNITED STATES
v.
WEBSTER M. SMITH, CADET, U.S. COAST GUARD
FILED UNDER SEAL[*]

MEMORANDUM ORDER AND OPINION FINDINGS OF FACT

During the summer training program at the start of their first class year, Cadet Smith and Cadet [SR] were both assigned to patrol boats that moored at Station Little Creek. Both lived in barracks rooms at the Station…she went on to state that on October 19th….**she agreed to pose for a picture with him in which both of them were nude, and later that night allowed him to perform cunnilingus on her then she performed fellatio on him.**

…. the Government's objection that this evidence is inadmissible in accordance with M.R.E. 413 [sic] is SUSTAINED.

EFFECTIVE DATE
This order was effective on 26 May 2006.
Done at Washington, DC,
/s/
Brian Judge
Captain, U.S. Coast Guard
Military Judge

Article 133. CONDUCT UNBECOMING AN OFFICE AND A LADY:

Any commissioned officer, cadet, or midshipman who is convicted of conduct unbecoming an officer and a lady or gentleman shall be punished as a court-martial may direct. (10 USC Sec. 933)

Sixth Amendment - Rights of Accused in Criminal Prosecutions

In all criminal prosecutions, the accused shall enjoy the right to a speedy and public trial, by an impartial jury of the State and district wherein the crime shall have been committed, which district shall have been previously ascertained by law, and to be informed of the nature and cause of the accusation; to be confronted with the witnesses against him; to have compulsory process for obtaining witnesses in his favor, and to have the Assistance of Counsel for his defense.

Decision of Supreme Court Without Comment Denying Certiorari

IN THE SUPREME COURT OF THE UNITED STATES OF
AMERICA
No. 10-18

Title:

Webster M. Smith, Petitioner
v.
United States

Docketed: June 30, 2010

Lower Ct: United States Court of Appeals for the Armed Forces

Case Nos.:(08-0719)

Decision Date: March 29, 2010

No. 10-   1 0 - 1 8   JUN 28 2010

IN THE

Supreme Court of the United States

WEBSTER M. SMITH,

Petitioner,

v.

UNITED STATES OF AMERICA,

Respondent.

ON PETITION FOR A WRIT OF CERTIORARI TO THE
UNITED STATES COURT OF APPEALS
FOR THE ARMED FORCES

PETITION FOR A WRIT OF CERTIORARI

DANIEL S. VOLCHOK
Counsel of Record
SETH P. WAXMAN
A. STEPHEN HUT, JR.
EDWARD C. DUMONT
WILMER CUTLER PICKERING
HALE AND DORR LLP
1875 Pennsylvania Avenue N.W.
Washington, D.C. 20006
(202) 663-6000
daniel.volchok@wilmerhale.com

No. 10-18

IN THE
SUPREME COURT OF THE UNITED STATES

WEBSTER M. SMITH,

Petitioner,

v.

THE UNITED STATES OF AMERICA,

Respondent,

ON PETITION FOR A WRIT OF CERTIORARI TO THE UNITED STATES COURT OF APPEALS FOR THE ARMED FORCES

BRIEF FOR AMICUS CURIAE, UNITED STATES ARMY DEFENSE APPELLATE DIVISION IN SUPPORT OF PETITIONER

MARK TELLITOCCI
Colonel, United States Army
Chief, Defense Appellate Division

JESS ROBERTS
Captain, United States Army
Appellate Counsel
Defense Appellate Division

JONATHAN POTTER
Lieutenant Colonel,
United States Army
Senior Appellate
Counsel
Defense Appellate
Division
901 N. Stuart Street
Arlington, VA 22203
(703) 588-6717
jonathan.potter@
conus.army.mil
Counsel of Record

2

"The white race deems itself to be the dominant race in this country. And so it is, in prestige, in achievement, in education, in wealth, and in power. So, I doubt not it will continue to be for all time, if it remains true to its great heritage and holds fast to the principles of constitutional liberty. But in view of the constitution, in the eyes of the law, there is in this country no superior, dominant, ruling class of citizens. There is no caste here. Our constitution is color-blind, and neither knows nor tolerates classes among citizens.... The destinies of the two races, in this country, are indissolubly linked together, and in the interests of both require that the common government of all shall not permit the seeds of race hate to be planted under the sanction of law."

-JUSTICE JOHN MARSHALL HARLAN
Dissenting in Plessy v. Ferguson, 1896

INTRODUCTION

We, as Americans, cherish fairness. We like to believe that people are not punished or unjustly rewarded without justifiable cause. We like to dwell on parables of white virtue and black advancement culminating in the flowering of goodwill all around. Events sometimes force us to widen our gaze and focus on terrain we would rather not see. The 2006 court-martial of Cadet Webster Smith at the United States Coast Guard Academy did just that. **The Webster Smith case was a litmus test for justice in America**. Every once in a while a case comes along that puts our humanity as a people, and as Americans, on trial. Everything that we profess to stand for as Americans was on trial. Our sense of justice in America and particularly in the U.S. Military was on trial. This was no ordinary trial. Our humanity was on trial. The Military Justice System was on trial. This case dissolved the deceptive façade and exposed certain moral deficiencies in our system of justice. This case alone puts the legitimacy of the entire military justice system at risk.

The American Criminal and Civil Justice Systems both failed Webster Smith. Nothing worked for him. None of the mechanisms designed to redress grievances rendered him a just result. A System is only as good as the people administering it.

Webster Smith availed himself of every path to justice that we have. He filed an Article 138 Complaint under the UCMJ. He faced the Article 32 Investigation with two lawyers. He asserted all of his Constitutional Criminal Guarantees. He knew and made appropriate use of the right to counsel, the right to remain silent, the right to a jury trial, the right to confront the witnesses against him, the right to call witnesses on his behalf, the right to present evidence favorable to him, the presumption of innocence until his guilt was proven beyond a reasonable doubt, and the right to argue his case before the jury.

His Appellate Counsel, Ronald Machen, was top notch. He became the United States Attorney for the District of Columbia. In April 2015, he left the position and returned to the law firm WilmerHale. **Wilmer Cutler Pickering Hale and Dorr®** has played a leading role in historic events and landmark cases that have shaped the nation and left their mark across the globe. In matters ranging from the Army-McCarthy hearings to the legal defense of civil rights, from the 9/11 Commission to the restoration of the rule of law in apartheid-torn South Africa, their lawyers have made contributions that have profoundly affected our society. Because the law is still a profession as well as a business, lawyers have special obligations to the administration of justice and the development of the law. Their lawyers are encouraged to meet these obligations through pro bono work. Attorney Machen represented Webster Smith on a pro bono basis. He received no fee.

Webster Smith appealed his conviction all the way to the United States Supreme Court. He lost at the Coast Guard Court of Criminal Appeals. He lost at the Court Of Appeals for the Armed Forces of the United States. The U. S. Supreme Court dismissed his appeal without comment. And, on top of the aforesaid, he filed a Complaint of Discrimination, pursuant to Commandant Instruction 5350.11. He had an air tight and fool proof case of disparate treatment. Yet, he lost. He lost because the System was manned by the most incompetent people God ever created. They did not have a clue as to what was going on in their office. The most significant case in the history of the Department of Homeland Security and the Armed Forces of America came to them and they were not capable of processing it properly.

On top of everything else, Webster Smith had bad luck. At some juncture along the way, most other people would have won, but not Webster Smith. One has to wonder why. There are some who will say that it was because he was Black. They will say that the System was designed and administered by white men and women; and, no Black man can obtain justice in that System. They might have a point, even

5

though some of the decisions made concerning this case were made by Black people in key offices.

In spite of all that, Webster Smith never played the Race Card. It was played, no doubt about it. It was played by the Superintendent and the Commandant of Cadets at the Coast Guard Academy. They played it subtly and superbly. They opened the game with the Race Card when they leaked his Official Cadet Portrait to the newspapers. That may not have been the beginning. It may have started when he was singled out months before for investigation and pursuit.

We now see that there is little or no justice in military justice. Any reasonable person who looks at this case or any other high profile military justice case would have to conclude that the Military Justice System is not designed to render justice. It is a system designed to punish. The entire courts-martial system, from Summary Court-martial to General Court-martial, has one specific purpose; that is to punish anyone who commits an offense against the Uniform Code of Military Justice.

This was not a rape case. Many senior Coast Guard officers tried to portray it as such. Webster Smith was not a rapist. He was not a sexual predator. His court-martial, with all of its faults, proved that this was not a rape case, and that Cadet Webster Smith was not a sexual predator.

Rape has occurred at the Coast Guard Academy and onboard the USCGC Eagle (WIX-327) as far back as 1977. From 1993 until the spring semester of 2005, the Coast Guard Academy (CGA) had 10 officially reported incidents of sexual misconduct, according to information provided by the Coast Guard Academy. There are rumors of other incidents of non-consensual sexual intercourse in the cadet living quarters of Chase Hall where the perpetrators were allowed to quietly resign their cadet appointments and simply disappear into the shadows.

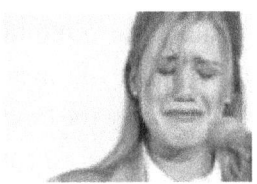

A former female Coast Guard Academy cadet, <u>Caitlin Stopper,</u> testified on Capitol Hill and told how her life became an "absolute hell" after she accused a fellow cadet of sexually assaulting her. Ms. Stopper said that Academy officials tried to blame her for the alleged attack. Her attacker was white. He was allowed to quietly resign his cadet appointment. He simply disappeared into the shadows. Her career was ruined; her life has never been the same.

According to a 2008 General Accounting Office (GAO) Report, from 2003 to 2006 there were <u>no </u>sexual-harassment complaints at the Coast Guard Academy, but there were 12 incidents of sexual assault reported to the Coast Guard Investigative Service (CGIS), with one incident in 2003, one in 2004, <u>none</u> in 2005 and 10 in 2006.

The 10 incidents reported in 2006 would appear to have occurred after the Webster Smith court-martial. Webster Smith was removed from the Chase Hall barracks in 2005. Who was doing all of the sexual assaulting in 2006? Why were none of those people brought to justice? They should have been given some form of discipline. It would have made it easier to understand why a General Court-martial, rather than a Summary Court-martial or an Article 15 Non-judicial Punishment, was necessary to punish Webster Smith.

Before the Webster Smith incident all cases involving allegations of sexual assault were quietly disposed of administratively. The rapists were all allowed to go quietly into the night. None of them were Black. This feeble attempt to make Webster Smith the poster child of Coast Guard Academy sexual assault is not worthy of the traditions of Hopley Yeaton, and the Long Blue Line of commissioned officers of the United States Coast Guard.

Hopley Yeaton was the first commissioned officer of the Revenue Cutter Service. The Revenue Marines were the forerunners of the modern Coast Guard. Yeaton was the commanding officer of the Revenue Service Cutter USRC Scammel. Yeaton probably took along his slave, Senegal, during the Scammel's patrols as this practice was permitted by the Treasury Department at that time. It would appear that the Coast Guard's attitude towards African Americans may have started on March 21, 1791 when Yeaton was commissioned by George Washington. His tomb now lies on the grounds of the Academy. In 1975 the Coast Guard cadets sailed the USCGC Eagle to Lubec, Maine where Yeaton's remains were exhumed. They were laid to rest at the Coast Guard Academy, not far from Hamilton Hall where Webster Smith was court-martialed.[1]

Webster Smith was not a sexual predator as he was called. He simply refused to stay on his side of the color-line. Apparently, someone felt that a message had to be sent; a lesson had to be taught. Just as East is East and West is West, and never the twain shall meet; the Coast Guard Academy was not going to become a breeding ground for miscegenation.

Until he was court-martialed, Webster Smith was a shining star in American society. He was a success. He had successfully competed for and won an appointment to one of the nation's premier military academies without the help of a congressional appointment. He was a good cadet, a good student, and a top flight athlete. He was six months away from graduating and becoming a commissioned officer in the United States Coast Guard. He was about to become a part of the system; but, out of the blue something terribly tragic happened. He received a wakeup call. He was told in no uncertain terms that his success, and his becoming a part of the establishment did not purchase for him what it had purchased for the white cadets. That is the equal protection of the law. If this was not a rape case, nor a sexual predator

---

[1] Hopley Yeaton, Wikipedia, the free encyclopedia

case, then one might be compelled to ask what kind of a case was it. Well, it would appear to have been a case of racial profiling. The Coast Guard was attempting to make Webster Smith the poster child of Coast Guard Academy sexual assaults. But the profile does not fit.

The Commandant of Cadets, Captain Douglas Wisniewski, addressed the corps of cadets and labeled Cadet Smith a sexual predator. Commander Ronald Bald, the prosecutor at the trial, described him as a manipulative senior who preyed on lonely women. They were attempting to build the profile of the Coast Guard Academy sexual predator. But former Cadet Webster Smith does not fit the profile. Later in this book I will give you the true profile of the Academy's sexual predator.

The Coast Guard Academy trains a group of cadets that others are encouraged to turn to if they are assaulted. Victims can also approach teachers or administrators. They can come forward anonymously or publicly and, according to the school's policies, are offered counseling and guidance whether they choose to have an investigation or not. This book will tell you what happened. It will tell you who did what to whom, but it will not tell you why. It cannot. The only people who know for certain have not been quoted in any media anywhere that I have been able to discover. It is left to you the reader to try to fathom why. This book contains all of the relevant facts. Any reasonable person should be able to conclude why Cadet Webster Smith was tried and punished by a General Court-martial. Applying a little bit of common sense and reflecting upon one's own life experiences in America should be sufficient to understand why Webster Smith was targeted.

The Year 2005 began like most others for Webster Smith with high hopes and lofty dreams. He was only one year away from his dream. In 2006 he was going to graduate from the Coast Guard Academy and realize his long cherished dream of becoming a Coast Guard commissioned officer just like his father, Cleon Smith, Coast Guard Academy Class of 1978.

But 2005 was a harbinger of unexpected tragedy for Webster Smith. Instead of graduating with honors in June 2006, he would be found guilty at a General Court-martial of multiple violations of the Uniform Code of Military Justice (UCMJ), sentenced to 6 months in jail, and kicked out of the Coast Guard.

At about 0200 on 4 December 2005 Officers at the direction of the Commandant of Cadets, CAPT Douglas Wisniewski entered his room in Chase Hall, and took him into custody. He was removed to a room in Munro Hall where he was interrogated by agents of the Coast Guard Investigative Service (CGIS).

Moreover, he was arbitrarily removed from academic training in December 2005 by the Commandant of Cadets and kept in that status for the entire semester. This was contrary to the provisions of Coast Guard Academy Regulations.

How could the charmed life of a cadet go so tragically wrong in only a few short months? The sense of loss of what might have been a brilliant career will follow us and the Coast Guard forever.

Webster Smith was the best and the brightest of what the minority community had to offer at that time. The court-martial of Webster Smith flies in the face of the Coast Guard's publically stated goals and official policies concerning minority recruitment. To have invested so much time and money in the recruitment and training of a superb athlete and a fine figure of a future officer, and then to court-martial him just a few weeks before graduation makes absolutely no sense; that is, unless he was sacrificed to send a message to America and the world.

The court-martial of Webster Smith separated Coast Guard history into two time periods, before and after. Just as the crucifixion of Jesus Christ split eternity into two parts, before and after; the court-martial of the first cadet in Coast Guard history left a permanent psychological marker in time.

The court-martial of a Black cadet marked a turning point for me in the way I think about my alma mater, the USCGA. When Webster Smith was court-martialed it felt like all the air had been sucked out of my universe. All my beautiful Coast Guard Academy memories were shattered. That world no longer afforded me peace and comfort. There was no harmony, nor tranquility left in that area of my memory banks.

Fundamentally life for cadets in Chase Hall has changed little since 1962 when the CGA opened its doors to the first Black cadet, Merle James Smith; yet, in many ways the Coast Guard Academy and the Coast Guard had become vastly different in 2006.

From 1962 until 1976 there were no female cadets at the Academy. Male and female cadets did not share adjacent rooms in Chase Hall. The notion of sexual contact between cadets was virtually unheard of. What we would do if a cadet got raped or became pregnant was not something for which we were formulating contingency plans. The idea of having a female Regimental Commander, or Commandant of Cadets, or a female Superintendent at the Academy was not even a figment in anyone's imagination.

In one generation after 1976, one out of every three cadets is a female. The number of Black cadets had remained low and marginal. Nevertheless, I still had faith in the senior officers leading the Coast Guard. I felt that they were competent and trustworthy. I had faith in the system.

Something died in my spirit when Webster Smith was court-martialed. When the appellate courts for the Coast Guard and the Armed Forces failed to overturn that conviction, it quashed the illusion that institutionalized racism was not alive and well in the military justice system. The court-martial of Webster Smith poses a fundamental challenge to my basic aim in my retired life as a former Coast Guard Law Specialist and Chief Minority Recruiter. My aim is to speak truth to power with love and understanding so that the quality of everyday life for military cadets is enhanced and institutionalized racism is stripped of its authority and legitimacy.

In a speech to Newsweek magazine correspondents in 1963, publisher Philip L. Graham described journalism as a "first rough draft of a history." Historians, like the general public, rely on journalists to get the story first, track down the leads, frame the issues, and shape public opinion about people and events. But journalists can only report on a small fragment of what happens on any given day. They concentrate on what they consider the most meaningful, unusual, or entertaining information; that is, stories that people want or ought to know about. Although the media seek to be a mirror of society, a mirror may distort according to the angle at which it is held. Also, a mirror may have blind spots.

Journalists strive to be objective, but their own backgrounds, experiences, and identities determine how they view the world, whom they choose to interview, what questions they ask (or do not ask), and how they interpret the facts they collect. The most insidious power that the news media has is the Power To Ignore. In their quest for news, the media have often ignored or overlooked significant events, ideas, and whole groups of people. Who reports the news and who writes history therefore makes a big difference.

For these reasons and others I closely followed the accounts of the Webster Smith case in the Associated Press (AP) articles and the reports coming out of New London, Connecticut in The Day newspaper. Also, since the achievements and failures of Black members of the Coast

Guard have largely been ignored, I decided to write an accurate account of the events surrounding the first court-martial of a cadet in Coast Guard history. Since that cadet happened to be an African American I felt it imperative that the account should be written by an African American academy graduate who happened to be a specialist in the law.

The astonishing disappearance of any mention of the Webster Smith Case from the public discourse and news reports of the Coast Guard Academy is an indication of how much the Coast Guard wants to forget that it ever used the Military Criminal Justice System to punish a cadet for conduct that has turned out to be more like teenage college pranks than like crimes under the Uniform Code of Military Justice.

Finally here is the full story. Now you can see the big picture. See who did what to whom, when, where and how. This is a story that is stranger than fiction, and more entertaining than a three ring circus.

See exactly what the cream of the is doing when they are not making the world safe for democracy. Here are ladies who can out drink, and out party the most salty old sea dogs. Here are young officer cadets that really know how to let their hair down.

When the sun goes down and the lights go out in Chase Hall that is when the real action begins. This is conduct in the worst traditions of hard working, hard drinking, and fast talking sailors. This is conduct unbecoming cadets, officers, gentlemen, and ladies.

And at the end of four years these cadets will graduate from the Academy ready to be worthy of the traditions of commissioned officers, gentlemen and ladies, in the service of their country and humanity.

Before moving on to the facts of The Webster Smith Story, let us consider one other anomaly. It appears that the Court of Appeals for the Armed Forces (CAAF) is able to see the obvious. Let us take a quick look at **United States v. Rogers**, a Coast Guard case ."This case shows that The United States Court of Appeals for the Armed Forces is willing to find error in a sexual assault conviction even in this political environment."

"Recently, the CAAF reversed a conviction for sexual assault in **Rogers.** This is an unpublished decision of the CAAF. The case was reversed because CAAF found that one of the panel members showed bias and the military judge failed to correct it.

In **Rogers,** appellant had been charged and convicted of numerous offenses, two of which were sexual assault of a person who was too intoxicated to consent. Prior to the trial, one of the female panel members was questioned regarding her beliefs about intoxication and consent.

The female panel member stated that it was her belief that "if you are so drunk that you can't remember giving consent, then you are too drunk to give consent." This belief is simply false, however, the military judge did not correct her. Additionally, the female panel member stated that she had some personal experiences with sexual assault, for example, her brother had been convicted of child molestation.

Defense challenged the panel member for both actual and implied bias based on these two things and the challenge was denied by the military judge. Therefore, the panel member remained on appellant's panel. Ultimately, Electrician's Mate Third Class Rogers was found guilty and sentenced to 10 years confinement, reduction to E-1, total forfeitures of all pay and allowances, and a bad conduct discharge.

He appealed his case to the Coast Guard Court of Criminal Appeals (CGCCA), however the court found no error and upheld the conviction. Then, CAAF granted the issue for review. CAAF unanimously held that the panel member's belief regarding consent was simply wrong and should have been corrected. Therefore, CAAF found that her false belief that being too drunk to remember means you are too drunk to consent constituted actual bias. Appellant's conviction and sentence were **reversed** due to this error. This case shows that CAAF is willing to find error in a sexual assault conviction even in this political environment.

The news media did not report anything concerning how the Jury was selected in the Webster Smith Case. We do not know how many prospective members were in the Jury Pool; or, how many were Voir Dired before the Jury Panel was seated. Neither do we know who conducted the Voir Dire, what kinds of questions were asked, whether the Defense Attorneys exercised any Peremptory Challenges or Challenges for Cause.

Webster Smith's Attorney on Appeal did not assert any issue related to the Voir Dire, or the selection process for the Members of the Jury. We are left to assume that no appealable issues were discovered concerning the Jury Selection Process. I only know that I would have had a field's day with the prospective members.

Picking the jury is a fun moment in a trial. Today picking a jury is so scientific. Professionals have preempted the process. They analyze and categorize prospective members based on their social profiles. The lawyers are told which prospective members are more likely to convict or who is more sympathetic to their theory of the case.

In the old days this was a relaxing part of the trial. Lawyers could engage the members in dialogue. The members could talk directly to the attorneys. This is the only time during a trial where such discourse is permitted. At all other times the members can only communicate with the attorneys through the Judge.

As a Trial Advocate there is no more personally fulfilling moment than picking a jury, unless you are lucky enough to have a "Perry Mason Moment". In court proceedings in the United States, **a Perry Mason moment** is said to have occurred whenever information is unexpectedly, and often dramatically, introduced into the record that changes the perception of the proceedings greatly and often influences the outcome. The evidence or other information, is usually unknown to most people present, and it is introduced into the record in a manner seen as determinative of the outcome of the proceedings regardless of whatever else occurs. The epitome would be where someone stands up and says 'I did it.'

It would be interesting to review the questionnaires submitted by the Prospective Members. Perhaps a FOIA Request to the Coast Guard Chief Counsel might get a favorable response. One thing for certain is that the Obama Administration has been the most secretive Government in the history of the United States. They for the most part do not grant FOIA requests, or they take forever to respond. When they do, everything is redacted, and the requester is usually hit with a hefty bill for reproduction and other services.

When I was prosecuting and defending in Coast Guard cases in San Francisco, the Military Judges usually did all the questioning of Prospective Members. There were two Trial Judges I remember most vividly. They were Captain Richard Applebaum and Captain James Meade. They liked to keep the Voir Dire short and to move the case along smartly.

CHAPTER 1

An American Tragedy

The Webster Smith Story is an American tragedy. It is not just the story of a Black Coast Guard Academy cadet; it is the story of an American family. It is the story of his mother, Belinda; and his father, Cleon; his wife, Lindsey and their daughter; and of his sister and brothers. It is the story of the friends of Webster Smith. They have all been harmed by the violence directed at their son, brother, husband, father and friend.

Webster Smith was born on July 9, 1983 in Houston, Texas. He is the oldest of four children born to Cleon and Belinda Smith. His sister attended the University of Texas at Arlington. The two younger brothers are twins and attended New Mexico Military Institute where one was in the Coast Guard Prep Program. He applied to the Coast Guard Academy but was denied after his brother was court-martialed.

Webster first distinguished himself in the 7th grade when he was inducted into the Honor Society. When he finished the 8th grade he was accepted into the Strake Jesuit Prep School. Before applying to the Coast Guard Academy (CGA) he attended a Navy Prep school. All of his instructors wrote letters of recommendation strongly in favor of his admission to CGA. To his classmates, teachers, and coaches at the Coast Guard Academy Webster Smith appeared to be a magnetic, charming and gifted young man, who had risen above his circumstances. Yet, in a moment, as if in the twinkling of an eye, a swift series of events diminished his popularity, vilified his name, and assailed his honor. His image was converted by senior Coast Guard officers from a popular athlete and nice guy to that of a sexual predator and public enemy number one at the Coast Guard Academy.

Snatched from his bed in Chase Hall in the middle of the night, he was whisked away to the barracks at the Groton Naval Submarine Base. He became an outcast from his friends and classmates. His dreams of a military career were dashed. He would not graduate from the Coast Guard Academy like his father. He stood up at his court-martial and proclaimed to the world that his greatest wish in life was to be a Coast Guard officer. Webster had dared to dream some big dreams. Like Alex Haley he had dared to believe that he could rise in the USCG to the highest level to which his talents and initiative could take him. Just like the Tuskegee Airmen and Navy World War II hero, Dorie Miller, he dared to dream that the time had come in America when a Black man could reach his full potential in the military. With energy and vitality he excelled in athletics and academics for three and a half years, before tragedy struck.

His parents were middle class African Americans. His father was a graduate of the Coast Guard Academy in the Class of 1978. There were 28 Black cadets in that class. One of the most distinguished members of that class was Vice Admiral Manson K. Brown, the first African American three star admiral in Coast Guard history. The Classes of 1977 and 1978 contained the largest numbers of Black freshmen cadets ever to enter the Academy in a single class. The Chief of the newly created Minority Recruiting Section (G-PMR-3) at Coast

Guard Headquarters traveled the dusty roads of America off the beaten path in search of qualified Black high school graduates who could make good Coast Guard officers. A few extremely gifted Black teenagers were given the chance to demonstrate their gifts. Webster Smith would not be permitted to further that legacy.

His mother, Belinda Ingram Smith, believed in God and a good education. After losing both parents as a teenager, she went on to become the Head Majorette of Winston-Salem State University (WSSU) a constituent institution of the University of North Carolina, and a historically Black public research university located in Winston-Salem, North Carolina. She accomplished this in her second year of college, something never before done by a sophomore. She left WSSU before receiving her undergraduate degree and went on to become the first Black female Crime Scene Investigator in the history of the Winston-Salem police Department.

This unbelievable turn about in what had been a Black success story is a singularly American tragedy. That a cadet so deeply respected and loved by his coaches and classmates could evoke such an outpouring of hate and anger from the senior officers at the Coast Guard Academy is a Coast Guard tragedy and an American tragedy.

(The African American cadets in the Coast Guard Academy Class of 1978. <u>Cleon Smith</u>, the father of Webster Smith, is pictured in the top row, extreme right. VADM Manson Brown is pictured above in the bottom row, extreme left.)(Circa June 1974)

CHAPTER 2

The Honor Concept

Unlike the other service academies, admission to USCGA is based solely upon merit and does not require a congressional nomination. Students are officers-in-training and are referred to as cadets. Tuition for cadets is fully funded by the Coast Guard in exchange for an obligation of 5 years active duty service upon graduation. This obligation increases if the cadet chooses to go to flight school or grad school. Approximately 400 cadets enter the academy each summer with about 200 cadets graduating. Graduates are commissioned as ensigns. The academic program grants a Bachelor of Science degree in one of eight majors, with a curriculum that grades cadets' performance upon a holistic education of academics, physical fitness, character and leadership. Cadets are required to adhere to the academy's Honor Concept, "Who lives here reveres honor, honors duty," which is emblazoned in the halls of the academy's entrance.

The Coast Guard Academy Cadet Handbook (2010) tells the new cadet recruit that when you take the oath of office as a Cadet in the United States Coast Guard you begin your development as a commissioned officer in the Armed Forces of the United States. You will be expected to protect and defend the Constitution of the United States and to selflessly serve the American people. America will place special trust and confidence in your integrity, ability and good character. This special trust and confidence must be earned. Make no mistake, the Academy leadership program is designed to challenge you. Swab Summer will test your self-discipline, your physical stamina, your commitment to service, and your capacity for teamwork. Above all, your success will depend on your daily commitment to the Coast Guard's Core Values of Honor, Respect, and Devotion to Duty.

The first seven weeks at the Coast Guard Academy are referred to as the Swab Summer Training Program. They are a period for training in military fundamentals and physical conditioning. They will prepare the "swabs" to join the Corps of Cadets at the start of the fall semester. In the Honor Concept there exists a higher standard of conduct that can neither be delineated by laws nor defined by regulations. It is the concept of Honor. Because Coast Guard cadets are called to a life of public service, and desire to attain that special trust and confidence which is placed in our nation's commissioned officers, their actions must be straightforward and always above reproach. As future law enforcement officers, each cadet's word and signature must be regarded as verification of the truth. The Coast Guard Academy's Honor Concept is exemplified by a person who will neither lie, cheat, steal, nor attempt to deceive. It is epitomized by an individual who places loyalty to duty above loyalty to personal friendship or to selfish desire. While the Coast Guard Academy's Honor Concept differs from a code, in that failure to report an honor offense is not itself an honor violation, cadets are required to report all activity that does not incriminate themselves. Moreover, the condoning of an honor violation is a Class I offense under the Cadet Regulations. Disenrollment is a very possible outcome. The Corps of Cadets are stewards of their Honor Concept. The following words are emblazoned in the tiling of Chase Hall's Quarterdeck, the cadet barracks' lobby: Who Lives Here, Reveres Honor, Honors Duty (The Coast Guard Academy Cadet Handbook (2010), p.13)

Military academies and universities across America send millions of young graduates into life each year with their heads stuffed with new ideas, technology, processes, perspectives, and maybe even a little practical experience they can use in their first assignment as newly commissioned officers. Only in a few schools has the person been so fundamentally transformed from the raw material received four years earlier as at a military academy such as the Coast Guard Academy. How does this happen?

When the future cadets arrive for Swab Summer, the vast majority are typical high school graduates. Most of them believe the sun rises and sets on them. By the end of the first week of Swab Summer, they understand this is not the liberal arts college where students wear uniforms they have expected. By the end of Swab Summer they are starting to learn that any value they have in this world is to be earned by their adherence to certain rules of behavior that bind them to each other as Coast Guard cadets and future officers.

At the center of their new world is adherence to a Cadet Honor Code to which they swear: "A cadet will not lie, cheat, or steal, nor tolerate those who do." Their whole new world is shaped around these principles. This initially shapeless reality begins to form into principles of rigid honesty, loyalty to their fellow cadets, and respect for their classmates and all with whom they associate.

Sometime between the end of their first year (Swab Year) and their Second Class Year when they will be expected to indoctrinate the new swabs, the majority start to understand the role of self discipline in riding the emotional waves of adolescence to a more settled understanding that the emotions are as changeable as the sea and not a reliable basis to govern personal behavior. Cadets learn to lead by first learning to follow. Basic Corps Values of honesty and loyalty become their template for acceptability. They develop a new understanding of the guiding role of honesty, truthfulness, and fairness in their world. Until this becomes second nature, a cadet is not prepared to lead, or to defend and to protect the Constitution of the United States of America.
George Washington, John Adams and Abraham Lincoln have all noted in one form or another that, "Our Constitution was made for a moral and religious people. It is wholly inadequate to the government of any other." Until we accept that as a nation, we are destined to continue to flail about rudderless in a tempestuous sea. (Business Ethics Articles

From The Honor Code, 2008 by Robert E. Freer, Jr., President, The Free Enterprise Foundation, and Visiting Professor, at The Citadel).

What is conduct unbecoming an officer and a lady? Does it violate the Honor Concept? Does conduct that violates the UCMJ constitute a higher standard than the Honor Concept? Times are changing so rapidly, one wonders if cadets and officers of today can be held to the same standards of conduct that were intended by the drafters of the UCMJ and the MCM promulgated in 1951? Not everyone can be expected to meet ideal moral standards, but how far can the standards of behavior of cadets and officers fall below contemporary community standards without seriously compromising their standing as officers and ladies? Have the changes in ethics and values of American society been reflected in the military?

Men and women behave differently today than they did sixty years ago. They relate differently to each other today than they did sixty years ago. Dishonorable conduct is magnified when it involves interpersonal relationships. Conduct that disgraces an individual personally and compromises her character may render that person unfit to be an officer. Making false statements, appearing intoxicated in public, failing to pay debts, reading another person's mail, using insulting or defamatory language, spreading rumors or gossip about another person, and associating with people known to engage in sexually immoral behavior do not carry the same stigma as they did sixty years ago. Homosexual conduct does not carry the stigma that it did sixty years ago. All of these types of behavior would have constituted behavior punishable by court-martial sixty years ago.

What type of conduct today would violate Article 133 of the UCMJ? Is consensual sodomy a violation of Article 133? Would violation of a cadet regulation be an offense under Article 133? Would engaging in consensual sex with an enlisted member of another branch of the armed forces while on temporary duty be a violation of Article 133 for which a cadet could be punished?

Could breach of a custom of the service result in a violation of Article 133? Many Coast Guard cadet customs have been adopted into the cadet regulations. "Sexual misconduct" at the USCGA is defined as "acts that disgrace or bring discredit on the Coast Guard or Coast Guard Academy and are sexual in nature", including lewd or lascivious acts, indecent exposure or homosexual conduct. But the definition also includes consensual acts that are prohibited in Chase Hall and on the Academy grounds, such as holding hands, kissing in public or having sex.

There are certain moral attributes common to the ideal cadet, officer, lady and gentleman. If a person commits acts of lewdness, dishonesty, indecency, lawlessness, indecorum, or violation of a cadet regulation that would seriously compromise her standing as a cadet or officer. Such conduct would at the very least be to the prejudice of good order and discipline in the armed forces.

Both the United States Military Academy and the United States Air Force Academy have adopted a **Cadet Honor Code** as a formalized statement of the minimum standard of ethics expected of cadets. Other military schools have similar codes with their own methods of administration. The United States Naval Academy, like the Coast Guard Academy, has a related standard, known as the Honor Concept.

West Point's Cadet Honor Code reads simply that:

"A cadet will not lie, cheat, steal, or tolerate those who do."

Cadets accused of violating the Honor Code face a standardized investigative and hearing process. If they are found guilty by a jury of their peers, they face severe consequences, up to and including expulsion from the Academy.

Definitions of the tenets of the Honor Code

LYING: Cadets violate the Honor Code by lying if they deliberately deceive another by stating an untruth or by any direct form of communication to include the telling of a partial truth and the vague or ambiguous use of information or language with the intent to deceive or mislead.

CHEATING: A violation of cheating would occur if a Cadet fraudulently acted out of self-interest or assisted another to do so with the intent to gain or to give an unfair advantage. Cheating includes such acts as plagiarism (presenting someone else's ideas, words, data, or work as one's own without documentation), misrepresentation (failing to document the assistance of another in the preparation, revision, or proofreading of an assignment), and using unauthorized notes.

STEALING: The wrongful taking, obtaining, or withholding by any means from the possession of the owner or any other person any money, personal property, article, or service of value of any kind, with intent to permanently deprive or defraud another person of the use and benefit of the property, or to appropriate it to either their own use or the use of any person other than the owner.

TOLERATION: Cadets violate the Honor Code by tolerating if they fail to report an unresolved incident with honor implications to proper authority within a reasonable length of time. "Proper authority" includes the Commandant, the Assistant Commandant, the Director of Military Training, the Athletic Director, a tactical officer, teacher or coach. A "reasonable length of time" is the time it takes to confront the Cadet candidate suspected of the honor violation and decide whether the incident was a misunderstanding or a possible violation of the Honor Code. A reasonable length of time is usually considered not to exceed 24 hours.

To have violated the honor code, a Cadet must have lied, cheated, stolen, or attempted to do so, or tolerated such action on the part of another Cadet. The procedural element of the Honor System examines the two elements that must be present for a Cadet to have committed an honor violation: the act and the intent to commit that act. The latter does not mean Intent to violate the Honor Code, but rather the Intent to commit the act itself.

Three rules of thumb

1. Does this action attempt to deceive anyone or allow anyone to be deceived?

2. Does this action gain or allow gain of a privilege or advantage to which I or someone else would not otherwise be entitled?

3. Would I be unsatisfied by the outcome if I were on the receiving end of this action?

U.S. Air Force Academy

The Cadet Honor Code at the Air Force Academy, like that at West Point, is the cornerstone of a cadet's professional training and development — the minimum standard of ethical conduct that cadets expect of themselves and their fellow cadets. Air Force's honor code was developed and adopted by the Class of 1959, the first class to graduate from the Academy, and has been handed down to every subsequent class. The code adopted was based largely on West Point's Honor Code, but was modified slightly to its current wording:

"We will not lie, steal, or cheat, nor tolerate among us anyone who does."

In 1984, the Cadet Wing voted to add an "Honor Oath," which was to be taken by all cadets. The oath is administered to fourth class cadets (freshmen) when they are formally accepted into the Wing at the conclusion of Basic Cadet Training. The oath remains unchanged since its adoption in 1984, and consists of a statement of the code, followed by a resolution to live honorably:

"We will not lie, steal or cheat, nor tolerate among us anyone who does. Furthermore, I resolve to do my duty and to live honorably, so help me God."

Cadets are considered the "guardians and stewards" of the Code. Cadet honor representatives throughout the Wing oversee the honor system by conducting education classes and investigating possible honor incidents. Cadets throughout the Wing are expected to sit on Honor Boards as juries that determine whether their fellow cadets violated the code. Cadets also recommend sanctions for violations. Although the presumed sanction for a violation is disenrollment, mitigating factors may result in the violator being placed in a probationary status for some period of time. This "honor probation" is usually only reserved for cadets in their first two years at the Academy. (Cadet Honor Code, from Wikipedia, the free encyclopedia)

Why have an honor code?

a) In professions such as the military where life is endangered by virtue of the institution's purpose, trust becomes sacred and integrity becomes a requisite quality for each professional. An officer who is not trustworthy cannot be tolerated; in some professions the cost of dishonesty is measured in dollars – in the Army, the cost is measured in human lives. The ability of West Point to educate, train and inspire outstanding leaders of character for our Army is predicated upon the functional necessity of honesty. In short, USMA expects its graduates and cadets to commit to a lifetime of honorable living.

b) In order to foster a genuine commitment to honorable living, USMA maintains Honor as a fundamental value. This value is operationalized through the Cadet Honor Code, the Honor Investigative and Hearing System, and the Honor Education System. Although the Honor Code & System "belongs" to West Point graduates, staff and faculty members, and cadets, the special charter of maintaining the Honor Code & System resides with the Corps of Cadets. Since 1922, the elected members of the Cadet Honor Committee have represented the Corps on all matters pertaining to honor and are the stewards of the Code. (Information Paper on "Honor" – A Bedrock of Military Leadership, USMA at West Point, **MACC-S- HON, 8 May 1998.**)

Spirit of the Code

a. The Cadet Honor Code describes the minimum standard of ethical behavior that all cadets have contracted to live by, not an abstract ideal to strive toward. Easy to understand and meet, it is the expected baseline behavior of cadets, not some ultimate state of purity that is hard to attain.

b. If the Code is the minimum standard for members of the Corps, what is the ideal that cadets should strive for?

c. That ideal is the "Spirit of the Code," an affirmation of the way of life that marks true leaders of character. The spirit of the code goes beyond the mere external adherence to rules. Rather, it is an expression of integrity and virtue springing from deep within and manifested in the actions of the honorable man or woman. Persons who accept the spirit of the code think of the Honor Code as a set of broad and fundamental principles, not as a list of prohibitions. In deciding to take any action, they ask if it is the right thing to do.

d. It is the Spirit of the Code that gives rise to the specific tenets of the Honor Code itself:

The spirit of the code embraces truthfulness in all its aspects. The Honor Code prohibits lying.
The spirit of the code calls for complete fairness in human relations. The Honor Code prohibits cheating.

The spirit of the code requires respect for the person and property of others. The Honor Code prohibits stealing.

The spirit of the code demands a personal commitment to upholding the ethical standards which gird the profession of arms. The Honor Code prohibits toleration of violations.

e. This, then, is the essence of the spirit of the code as it applies to cadets - a cadet is truthful, fair, respectful of others' property, and committed to maintaining ethical standards in the Corps. This spirit shapes not only West Point but sets the ethical standards for leadership in the Army itself.

f. The growth of each cadet as a leader of character is marked by strict adherence to the minimum standards of the code, combined with a driving desire to progress beyond the external standards to an internalization of the spirit of the code. That is expected by the Corps, by the Long Gray Line, and by the nation.

How does the Honor Code operate? (At the **U. S. Air Force Academy**)

The administration of the Honor Code is accomplished by a joint effort between cadets and Academy officers. Each possible Honor Code violation is thoroughly investigated on the premise that the accused cadet is honorable until a sufficient amount of reasonable evidence shows otherwise. The primary sanction for code violations is dismissal from the Academy. Some cadets, however, are retained on probationary status. The main concern in the administration of the code is that fairness and equity be maintained while teaching the importance of personal responsibility and that the rights of the cadets are fully protected during this process. Cadets are taught the specifics of the administration of the Honor Code during Basic Cadet Training and throughout their Academy experience.

Cadets who live under the Honor Code agree it is a vital part of their development as military professionals. It also represents a broader aspect of ethical maturity which will serve them throughout their lives. As the bearers of the public trust, both as cadets and as officers, it is the Honor Code which helps build a personal integrity able to withstand the rigorous demands placed upon them. (The Honor Code, printable fact sheet, USAFA).

CHAPTER 3

Before The Court-martial

On December 4, 2005 an officer on duty at the United States Coast Guard Academy (USCGA) received an allegation of sexual misconduct from a cadet, setting off an inquiry by the Coast Guard Investigative Services (CGIS), based in Washington, D.C.. The Commandant of Cadets, Captain Douglas Wisniewski, took immediate action to initiate an investigation into these allegations.

"Sexual misconduct" at the USCGA is defined as "acts that disgrace or bring discredit on the Coast Guard or Coast Guard Academy and are sexual in nature", including lewd or lascivious acts, indecent exposure or homosexual conduct. But the definition also includes consensual acts that are prohibited on Academy grounds, such as holding hands, kissing in public or having sex.

From 1993 until the spring semester of 2005, the Coast Guard Academy had 10 reported incidents of sexual misconduct, according to information provided by the CGA. Of those, six incidents resulted in dismissal of the accused and two ended in resignation. In the remaining two cases, there was insufficient evidence to pursue charges. No action was taken against the accused.

The Coast Guard Academy had 982 cadets, nearly 30 percent of whom were women in 2005. One out of every three cadets was a female.

In the USCGA the torch had passed to a new gender. Women represent about 30 percent of CGA cadets, compared with less than 20 percent at the Air Force and Naval Academies and about 15 percent at West Point, the Army Academy.

Cadet First Class Webster Smith was charged with sexually assaulting six female cadets in Chase Hall, the cadet living quarters, and in other locations. Cadet Smith was separated from the corps of cadets after the first complaint was filed on 4 December 2005. He was placed in pre-trial confinement and made to perform hard labor. No charges had been filed against him; but he was confined, forced to work at hard labor on the boat docks during the day, and forbidden to attempt any form of communications with his friends in Chase Hall. He could not go to class to continue his academic studies or eat in the cadet ward room. At night he was transported to the Navy enlisted men's barracks at Groton Naval Submarine Base across the Thames River from the USCGA.

He was not placed in protective custody. No threats had been made against his safety. It was feared that any contact with the potential government witnesses against him would jeopardize the case the Administration was trying to build. No justification was given for these draconian measures.

Smith, a linebacker on the Academy's football team, was charged 9 February 2006 under the Uniform Code Of Military Justice (UCMJ) with rape, assault, indecent assault and sodomy with female cadets. He had served about two months of pre-trial confinement before any charges had been preferred against him.

When I first heard that Admiral James Van Sice, the Academy Superintendent, was considering convening a court-martial to punish a CGA cadet, I was flabbergasted. After much soul searching, I decided to write him a letter.

In my letter to Admiral James Van Sice, the Superintendent of the United States Coast Guard Academy, and the man who convened the court-martial that tried Cadet Webster Smith for a long list of sex crimes, this is what I said:

February 2006

Dear Admiral Van Sice,

I think a great travesty of justice has been committed. It appears that a gross miscarriage of justice has been done at the Coast Guard Academy. What I cannot figure out is was it done ignorantly or by design. How do you frame a man, rig a court-martial, and commit the greatest travesty in the history of the Academy in broad daylight with the whole world watching? With bravado, that's how.

The first thing that you do is, you pick the lawyer for the accused. Then you give the lawyer a medal, something of distinction, like the Coast Guard Achievement Medal. And you select someone who was on the Coast Guard Academy board of Control, and someone you appointed to the Board of Directors of the Coast Guard Foundation. You do not want anyone who might be too independent of the Coast Guard Academy. You make sure that you choose someone with broad corporate law experience, someone with broad experience in negotiating and drafting contracts, someone like the former General Counsel for General Dynamic Electric Boat. And you be sure that he has limited or no experience in criminal law, and trial and defense work, someone not very comfortable in a criminal court room.

Then you refuse to give the accused a Coast Guard Detailed Military Counsel, because you know that a Coast Guard lawyer might have too much ethical integrity to go along with the travesty. So, you look around and you find an Individual Military Counsel from the JAG Corps of the Navy. You want someone not familiar with the Coast Guard Rules of Practice and Procedure and the Local Rules. You want someone that you can control, not someone who will swear charges against a prosecution witness who gives self-incriminating testimony at trial without a Grant of Immunity, either Transactional or Testimonial. Also, you need someone who will not ask to see the written Grants of Immunity and have them admitted into the Record as exhibits.

Also, you need someone who will not prepare for the trial. It would not be convenient if he brought a lot of Pre-Trial motions to suppress testimony and Motions In Limine to prevent prosecution behavior that would be prejudicial to the Defendant, like newly commissioned officers being allowed to testify in Ensign uniforms while the accused is wearing cadet garb.

When you schedule the trial is important. In order to give leverage and unfair advantage to the prosecution witness, you wait until after graduation, so that the prosecution has a parade of newly commissioned officers to testify against the cadet.

Then you have to agree not to charge the prosecution witness for crimes against the Uniform Code of Military Justice that you know they committed with Webster Smith. It would be difficult to commit sodomy alone. So both participants would be equally guilty. During their testimony all of the female witnesses gave declaration against their interests and made self-incriminating statements.

And you know that under the UCMJ, anyone can swear charges against anyone else. A seaman can swear charges against an admiral, or a private against a general. Even Webster Smith could swear charges against all of the witnesses against him and those charges have to be disposed of in due process.

That is another reason why you must choose the attorney for the accused very carefully. You do not want him swearing charges against the prosecution witnesses who have no immunity from prosecution. It is still not too late.

Next, at trial you give no Article 31 Warnings. Not a single reporter reported that the witnesses had attorneys or that they were warned. They had to be told that they were suspected of having committed an offense under the UCMJ, that they had a right to remain silent, that anything they said could be used against them in a court of law. Not to warn a person whom you suspect is guilty of a crime under the UCMJ before asking them any questions is a violation of the UCMJ.

Not to put this information before the jury was procedural error. Not one newspaper reported that this information was given to the jurors. If it had been done someone would have reported it. Even non-legal trained reporters know how to report facts whether they seem important to them or not.

If you did what I think you did, you may be subject to charges under the Uniform Code of Military Justice for dereliction of duty. If you did not give the witnesses who testified against Webster Smith grants of immunity, and you allowed them to testify on the record, under oath, and give incriminating statements, without giving them Article 31 warnings, then you have violated the UCMJ. Also, the Defense Team would have had to be given copies of the Grant of Immunity, and the Jury would have had to be told that the witness was testifying under a Grant of Immunity, because that is a factor in judging the credibility of the witness.

Nowhere was it reported that the witnesses came into court with their own lawyers. That would have indicated that they had not been granted immunity from prosecution. Nowhere was it reported that the witnesses were given Article 31 warnings. At least one reporter would have picked up on that. That is a very relevant and important fact.

I cannot believe that you did what I think you did. That would mean that you were running a Three Ring Circus. It may turn out that you guys are the new Gang That Could Not Shoot Straight.

If you allowed those females to testify to things that they engaged in with Webster Smith, things that were violations of the UCMJ, and were not given their own Detailed Military Counsel, and were not given written Grants of Immunity, then they have incriminated themselves and are subject to prosecution under the UCMJ. Since you convened a court-martial to try Webster Smith, then you are duty bound to swear out charges against every woman who testified that she engaged in sodomy, public drunkenness, and conduct unbecoming an officer and gentleperson, among other things.

We are a nation of laws, and Webster Smith was entitled to the equal protection of the law. The Constitution of the United States guarantees him that. When you decided to prosecute him only and not his equally culpable partners for sodomy, you denied him the equal protection of the law. That was a gross violation of his civil rights. Also, if you granted the women immunity and not Webster Smith, then you had better have had a very good reason that will withstand Constitutional scrutiny. Moreover, if you allowed those women to testify under oath, on the record, without any Article 31 warnings, and no grant of full immunity, you placed them in jeopardy. You may have ruined all of their lives.

I am going to allow you and the Commandant (G-L) and Commandant (G-P) time to straighten out this mess. If you do not, I will refer it to the NAACP Legal Defense Fund, Inc. Then I will contact the Congressional Black Caucus, and Webster Smith's senators from Texas, and the Civil Rights Division of the Justice Department to ask them to start an investigation to see if any of Cadet Webster Smith's civil rights were violated.

/s/

L. Steverson

LCDR, U. S. Coast Guard (Retired)

The Article 32 Investigation

The Article 32 Investigation was convened on March 21, 2006 to determine whether there was probable cause to convene a court-martial to prosecute the charges. The Investigating Officer received the testimony of seven female cadets who accused Cadet Smith of assaulting them between May and November 2005.

The USCGA Superintendent, Admiral James Van Sice, was the Convening Authority.

Before cadet Webster Smith could be court-martialed an Article 32 Investigation was required to determine if there was probable cause to believe that a crime under the UCMJ had been committed. It is the military equivalent of a grand jury. The Article 32 Investigating Officer was <u>Commander Steven Anderson</u>. Navy Midshipman Kristin Strizki (KS) was among the final witnesses for the government at the Article 32 hearing.

Five female Coast Guard Academy cadets, who were alleged victims, testified in secret at the Article 32 hearing. KS testified in public. She testified that the two Coast Guard cadets, Smith and KN, were visiting her in Annapolis, Maryland, when they began drinking at an off-campus house. She said KN passed out after consuming more than 2 liters of wine and two beers. The next morning, Smith suggested KS take her friend to get the morning-after pill, she said. KS said her friend had no recollection of having sex with Smith and confronted him. "He said, 'Oh please, you wanted it,'" she testified. "That's when she said, 'There is no way in hell I would have wanted to have sex with you last night, even if I was sober.'"

Another witness, Coast Guard cadet Jere Cherni, testified that the alleged victim became pregnant and underwent an operation that she felt was immoral. After objections from Smith's attorneys, Cherni was not permitted to specify the operation.

After hearing all of the evidence, CDR Anderson **made a recommendation to the Convening Authority that the charge of rape**

NOT be referred to a General Court-martial. That was like a Grand Jury that refused to indict. It refused to return a true bill of indictment. The District Attorney, at that point, would be foolish to waste the taxpayers' money pursuing charges that were not legally supportable and that he could not prove. The only reason for going ahead in spite of the failure to indict would have been if he had a personal vendetta against the accused or a political motive.

The Article 32 Investigating Officer did not feel that there was sufficient evidence to support the charge. Admiral Van Sice, Captain Wisniewski, and Commander Sean Gill rejected the recommendation of the Article 32 Investigating Officer and referred the charge of rape to a General Court-martial. Admiral Van Sice and Captain Doug Wisniewski were not concerned about wasting the taxpayers' money; nor were they worried about being re-elected. They were secure in their positions, and they appeared to have been blinded by rage and other more revolting motives. They were in a position of public trust. Any reasonable person would have had to question their judgment. All of the cadets at the Academy are in their care for safekeeping and nurturing. They did not hesitate to sacrifice this innocent young cadet for some sinister ulterior motive. Who were they trying to impress?

Judge Paul Weil, a Federal Administrative Law Judge (ALJ) who decided many discrimination cases for the Department of Transportation, wrote a long time ago in one of his decision that the Coast Guard has a long history of not dealing fairly with its Black personnel and officers. No one told Webster Smith's parents that fact before they entrusted their precious son to the Coast Guard Academy's Commandant of Cadets.

The Article 32 Investigating Officer was correct in his assessment. At the Trial Cadet Webster Smith was found **not guilty of raping** his girlfriend, Cadet KN. He was found guilty of extorting sexual favors from **Cadet SR**. These charges were added at the last minute, but Cadet SR **lied** through her teeth. It was alleged that Webster Smith was holding **a secret** over SR that she was afraid would ruin her career if revealed. At the Trial no one seemed to want to know what the so-called secret was. Well, the secret was that she was having torrid sex with a Navy enlisted man in Virginia the previous summer.

Webster Smith never revealed her secret. He did not even tell his mother and father. They had not been able to speak to him. He was being held off base without any contact with anyone, except his lawyers. **He did not extort SR for sexual favors. She extorted him and lied about it under oath.**

On 19 October 2005 SR sent Webster Smith 3 text messages. Each time she asked him to come to her room. The first time he came to her room, she reminded him of their conversation in Virginia the previous summer, when they fantasized about taking nude photos of each other. Webster did not bring a camera to her room, but she was ready with her camera. They took nude photos of each other with her camera, and he left. There was no touching and there was no sex.

When Webster Smith returned to his room, SR text messaged him a second time, and asked him to come back. When he arrived the second time, SR offered to give him a back massage. When she had finished, he offered to return the favor. They both had their clothes on, but she later alleged that he touched her breast. They did not engage in any sexual acts. Smith went back to his room.

Cadet SR sent him a third text message asking him to come back to her room a third time. She said her legs were sore. Smith massaged her legs and they both got turned on resulting in his performing oral sex on her. When he was finished he stood up to leave. That is when she reached out and grabbed him by his belt and pulled him back to her. She unzipped his fly and took out his penis. He stopped her. He told her that she did not have to do that just because he had serviced her. She said "Yeah, right!" And she proceeded to perform oral sex on him. Then he left.

That does not sound very much like extortion. Extortion should be made of sterner stuff. If SR had been extorted or coerced in any way, why did she call him back two more times? Did she later tell a lie of her own volition or was she coached?

The three sexual encounters occurred in her room on 19 October 2005. Nothing was ever mentioned concerning the events of that night until March of 2006, six months later. When SR was told that her friends needed her help, she told of the events of that night. They told her that they were looking for anyone who had had any sexual involvement with Webster Smith. The events were turned around just enough so that it would seem that Webster Smith had taken advantage of her. He had not. He was a victim of a malicious campaign of lies. A conspiracy had been hatched. The foul deed was in the making. Poor trusting good friend Webster Smith was being duped.

At a Pre-trial hearing, before the Jury was seated, when Cadet SR was called to testify in a motion's session, **she pleaded the 5th Amendment**. She refused to testify on the grounds that she might be incriminated. Later, at trial, she testified, and she lied. No media reported that she had been given her Article 31 (right against self-incrimination) Rights, but she testified. What happened between the Pre-trial Hearing and the trial in front of the jury? Did she make a deal with the Prosecutor and the Convening Authority?

No one reported in any media that she was given a grant of immunity. No written Grant of Immunity was admitted into evidence, or shown to the jury. What happened? Even the lies she told incriminated her. The charges involving her are the only charges that Webster Smith was found guilty of, except for one other. That was disobedience of an order. The order was not to send any Email messages to his friend at The Naval Academy at Annapolis, MD.. He sent one Email to his friend. For that he was found guilty of disobedience of an order. That seems awfully petty.

These childish pranks had landed him in jail. The lies of an unscrupulous woman and sending an Email to a friend ended his career and sent him to jail. It ruined a perfect life. He had never received as much as one demerit in his life. All through Navy Prep School he had

41

not received one demerit. All through three and a half years at the Coast Guard Academy, he had not received one demerit. He was on the Regimental Command Staff the previous summer.

When he ran afoul of Captain Doug Wisniewski and divulged KN's abortion secret his military career was over. All it took was a few lies, a few naive and promiscuous young females, and a very angry, ruthless, and powerful captain. This was an abuse of process. To go against the Article 32 Officer's recommendation was an abuse of discretion. To suborn frightened young girls to give biased and slanted testimony was an abuse of the prestige of the Academy. To use the Military Justice apparatus for his own personal vendetta was an abuse of process.

CDR Gill felt that the girls were **"up to it"**; so, he offered his non-trial experience against CDR Andersen's trial experience and persuaded Admiral Van Sice to go ahead with a general court-martial. He felt that there was the barest scintilla of evidence of rape, and that there was a very thin chance that they could convince a jury of fellow officers to vote for a conviction. He was flat-out wrong to do that. Yet, he has remained in the shadows all this time. Like most people who give bad advice, he does not want to receive credit for it. That is the trouble with free advice; you get what you paid for.

CDR Gill was also the person responsible for ensuring that none of the females involved received any disciplinary action. It was, no doubt, his advice to give immunity from prosecution to any female who would stand up and give testimony against Webster Smith. As charge after charge was dismissed prior to trial based on defense motions, it was CDR Gill who kept rounding up new witnesses and new allegations after the court-martial had begun. Sixteen or more charges and specifications were dismissed during preliminary motions sessions. CDR Gill was able to roundup **Shelly Raudenbush (SR)** at the last minute. It was her coached testimony that gave CDR Gill and CAPT Wisniewski and ADM Van Sice the conviction that they sought.

And that is why she was protected. She was shielded from cross-examination. She was granted immunity. The Trial counsel, prosecutor, CDR Bald, had been investigating the case from the beginning, since 2005 with CDR Gill. They wanted to build a wall of protection around her. The jury heard nothing about her prior bad acts or her patterns of behavior in other similar situations. The Military Judge at trial, **CAPTAIN Brian Judge**, was handpicked, so he went along with it all.

Commander Sean Gill, the Academy Staff Judge Advocate, had been involved in this case before the CGIS investigation in 2006. Commander Gill had been conducting his own investigation since 2005, at the request of CAPT Wisniewski and ADM Van Sice. He was not at all fond of Webster Smith. In point of fact, he had a great dislike for him. He should have been prevented from having any official role with respect to this case. He had been interviewing female cadets who had dated Webster Smith socially. They had confided in him. They told him that they thought Webster Smith would be upset if he knew that they had come forward. He solicited the assistance of **Commander Ronald Bald** in his investigation before there was a charge sheet and before the Article 32 was convened.

.CDR Ronald Bald would later serve as the Prosecutor at the court-martial. CDR Gill argued strongly against non-judicial punishment and any lesser criminal forum, such as a Summary or Special Court-martial, because he had obtained the solemn guarantee from several female cadets that they would testify at a court-martial. He was only able to get their cooperation by promising them that Webster Smith would be sent away for a long time. He promised long jail time, and he promised to get Webster Smith out of the cadet barracks immediately. He was the one who persuade CAPT Wisniewski to snatch Cadet Webster Smith out of the barracks at midnight in handcuffs and send him to the Navy barracks at Groton. Then he was not allowed to attend classes where he would come into contact with any of the potential female witnesses. That would have unraveled Cdr Gill's plans for a court-martial. Instead, Webster Smith was forced to work at hard labor at the boat docks as they continued to try to build a case against him.

A revealing account in the Navy Times concerning testimony at the trial adds some more background: Smith's former girlfriend (KN) testified on the opening day of the court-martial that on the night when she and Smith traveled to the Naval Academy at Annapolis she blacked out early and learned the next morning that she and Smith had had sex. Smith told her the condom had broken and recommended she seek emergency contraception, but she did not know whether to believe him, she said. She also said she couldn't remember details about that morning, including what she was wearing or whether she looked for physical evidence indicating they'd had sex. Weeks later, she took a home pregnancy test.

> "When did you realize that the accused had actually had sex with you?" asked CDR Ronald Bald, the military prosecutor.
> "When I saw the positive result on the pregnancy test," she said.
> "What did you think had happened?" Bald asked.
> "I thought that I had been date-raped," she replied.

Yet their relationship continued. The night after the rape allegedly occurred, the witness acknowledged, she and Smith attended a concert with friends and then spent the night together in a hotel.
Testimony during pretrial hearings suggested that KN had had an abortion, but the military judge refused to allow any medical records into evidence on June 20, saying it would prejudice the jury. Jurors were told only that KN did not carry the child to term.

Smith and KN remained close even after they returned to the Coast Guard Academy, she said. They continued to exchange affectionate e-mails and continued seeing each other for dinner. Months after the rape allegedly occurred, she said, they had sex in his car. And while prosecutors say Smith was a controlling, emotionally abusive boyfriend, one of Smith's friends testified that KN was equally to blame.

The friend testified that she was watching a movie with Smith the year before when KN, the girlfriend, walked in and said "How could you do that to me? How could you steal him from me," the witness, Bazinet recalled KN yelling. "It was scary", she testified. She and KN were classmates.

Smith's military defense lawyer, Lt. Stuart Kirkby, stressed there was no DNA, no forensic evidence, no rape kit and no crime scene photos. He said the former girlfriend "doesn't recall anything from the moment she left the house, conveniently, until the very next morning." Defense attorneys maintained that KN was not as drunk as she said and suggested that she may have concocted the rape accusation to cover up her embarrassment at having sex with an on-again, off-again boyfriend.

When Smith took the witness stand he testified that he and KN had some drinks and went to a bar. She gave him a look, he said, and they went out to the car, where he said they had consensual sex. She got sick after they had sex, he said, but when they got home, she was able to walk to bed. He said they had sex again the next morning and evening.

What began as a trial against an accused sexual predator ended looking more like a series of murky encounters between college students, with consent often clouded by alcohol. But the case also offered a rare and often unflattering glimpse at cadet life. Two of Smith's four accusers testified that they didn't believe sexual assault was understood or taken seriously enough on campus. Another said she felt alone, unable to explain her situation. And Capt. Douglas Wisniewski, the departing Commandant of Cadets, described fear and suspicion in the student body, saying some female cadets were hesitant to come forward with assault allegations, a culture that Wisniewski spent months denying existed.

"Clearly this needs to be a moment of change at the Coast Guard Academy," said U.S. Rep. Rosa DeLauro, D-Conn., who proposed a federal review of the school's sexual assault policies.

CHAPTER 4

Webster Smith Filed An Article 138 Complaint

Article 138 is one of the most powerful rights under the Uniform Code of Military Justice (UCMJ), but it is one of the rights least known and least used by military personnel. Under Article 138 of the UCMJ, "any member of the armed forces who believes himself (or herself) wronged by his (or her) commanding officer" may request redress. If such redress is refused, a complaint may be made and a superior officer must "examine into the complaint."

Article 138 of the Uniform Code of Military Justice (UCMJ) gives every member of the Armed Forces the right to complain that he or she was wronged by his or her commanding officer. The right even extends to those subject to the UCMJ on inactive duty for training.)
Cadet Webster Smith filed an Article 138 Complaint against Captain Douglas Wisniewski. There is no record of it having been resolved.

ART. 138 of the UCMJ: COMPLAINTS OF WRONGS

Any member of the armed forces who believes himself wronged by his commanding officer, and who, upon due application to that commanding officer, is refused redress, may complain to any superior commissioned officer, who shall foreword the complaint to the office exercising court-martial jurisdiction over the officer against whom it is made. The officer exercising general court-martial jurisdiction shall examine into the complaint and take proper measures for redressing the wrong complained of; and he shall, as soon as possible, send to the Secretary concerned a true statement of that complaint, with the proceedings thereon.

Matters appropriate to address under Article 138 include discretionary acts or omissions by a commander that adversely affect the member personally and are:

> In violation of law or regulation
> Beyond the legitimate authority of that commander
> Arbitrary, capricious, or an abuse of discretion, or
> Clearly unfair (e.g., selective application of standards).
> Procedures for filing complaint.

Within 90 days (180 days for the Air Force) of the alleged wrong, the member submits his or her complaint in writing, along with supporting evidence, to the commander alleged to have committed the wrong. There is no specific written format for an Article 138 complaint, but it should be in normal military letter format, and should clearly state that it is a complaint under the provisions of Article 138 of the Uniform Code of Military Justice.

The commander receiving the complaint must promptly notify the complainant in writing whether the demand for redress is granted or denied.

The reply must state the basis for denying the requested relief. The commander may consider additional evidence and must attach a copy of the additional evidence to the file.

If the commander refuses to grant the requested relief, the member may submit the complaint, along with the commander's response, to ANY SUPERIOR COMMISSIONED OFFICER, who is

MANDATED to forward the complaint to the officer exercising General Court-Martial Convening Authority (GCMCA) over the commander being complained about. The officer may attach additional pertinent documentary evidence and comment on availability of witnesses or evidence, but may not comment on the merits of the complaint.

(Special Note: Article 138 clearly states that complaints may be addressed to any superior commissioned officer. However, only the Air Force regulations allow the complainant to bypass their chain of command when filing a complaint. The Army requires that the complaint be filed with the "complainant's immediate superior commissioned officer." A complaint in the Navy or Marine Corps must be submitted "via the chain of command, including the respondent." Before reaching the general court-martial convening authority, an intermediate officer "to whom a complaint is forwarded" may "comment on the merits of the complaint, add pertinent evidentiary material to the file, and, if empowered to do so, grant redress." In the Air Force, the complainant may "submit the claim directly, or through any superior commissioned officer" to the general court-martial convening authority).

GCMCA's Responsibilities

Conduct or direct further investigation of the matter, as appropriate.

Notify the complainant, in writing, of the action taken on the complaint and the reasons for such action.

Refer the complainant to appropriate channels that exist specifically to address the alleged wrongs (i.e., performance reports, suspension from flying status, assessment of pecuniary liability). This referral constitutes final action.

Retain two complete copies of the file, and return the originals to the complainant.

After taking final action, forward a copy of the complete file to the Secretary of the Service (i.e., Secretary of the Army, Secretary of the Air Force, etc.), for final approval/disposition.

The GCMCA is prohibited from delegating his or her responsibilities to act on complaints submitted pursuant to Article 138.

Matters outside the scope of the Article 138 complaint process

Acts or omissions affecting the member which were not initiated or ratified by the commander

Disciplinary action under the UCMJ, including non-judicial punishment under Article 15 (however, deferral of post-trial confinement is within scope of Article 138)

Actions initiated against the member where the governing directive requires final action by the Office of the Secretary of the Service

Complaints against the GCMCA related to the resolution of an Article 138 complaint (except for alleging the GCMCA failed to forward a copy of the file to the Secretary of the Service)

Complaints seeking disciplinary action against another

Situations where procedures exist that provide "the individual notice of an action, a right to rebut, or a hearing" and "review by an authority superior to the officer originating the action." (This includes most administrative boards)

9 MAY 2006

To: Superintendent, U.S. Coast Guard Academy
From: Cadet 1/C Webster Smith
Subj: Article 138 Complaint

At about 0200 on 12/4/05 Officers at the direction of the
Commandant of Cadets, CAPT Wisniewski entered my room at
Chase Hall, took me into custody and removed me to a room in
Munro Hall. I was held there, ordered not to leave and was
interrogated by Coast Guard Intelligence Investigators twice over
the next several days regarding allegations that I had raped
certain female cadets.

From the date of my arrest, I was specifically directed not to
have contact with other cadets either through personal
interaction, telephone or communication via computer. I was
forbidden to go to classes but was brought my books such that I
could complete remaining work for the academic term.

On 12/16/05, I was allowed to go home to Texas on leave with
certain restrictions preserved from the earlier conditions,
particularly no contact with any of the Corps of Cadets and I was
further restricted from coming within 100 miles of the Academy
without specific authorization. I continued in that status until
February 14, when I returned to New London to face charges for
violations of the UCMJ, filed on February 14.

It had been my fond hope that I could return to training at the
Academy. Discussion, in mid-January, between the Commandant
of Cadets and my Father, Cleon Smith, indicated that might be
likely. In phone discussions between CAPT Wisniewski, my
Father and me on Friday 27 January, the Commandant of Cadets

made it very clear that he did not intend on bringing me back to the Academy any time soon. He seemed to attribute that to the investigation on sexual misconduct continuing. When asked, he refused to identify any ways that I was considered a threat to the continuance of that activity but allowed that he did not feel that I would continue with my Academy Class. This was quite disturbing because my Father and I felt that I should be brought under whatever restrictive order and directions as appropriate but I could resume my military duties and continue my training. CAPT. Wisniewski refused to consider this option. My Father responded that he felt obligated to raise this issue to another level.

On my behalf, CDR Merle Smith, USCGR (Ret.) attempted to get an appointment with Admiral Van Sice. CAPT Thomas, the Assistant Superintendent, returned that call on 1 February, 2006. He inquired as to the subject of the desired meeting and CDR Smith's role. CDR Smith identified that he was acting in the role of my counsel. CAPT Thomas expressed concern regarding such a meeting with ADM Van Sice being the Convening Authority, while investigation was being conducted and that he would have to check with the lawyers. CDR Smith pointed out that the Admiral was also the Convening Authority for the purpose of Article 138 complaints and that was the reason for his request. CAPT Thomas said that he would review the matter with the lawyers and get back to him. No further contact was initiated by Academy staff until 8 February, when LT Sanders, my Company Officer called to advise me that charges had been prepared and he would fax them to me.

Upon review, we went from no reason for me to be brought back and just sit for some undeterminable period of time (1/27/06), to a request to meet with the Admiral to discuss Article 138 related issues (2/1/06), to 16 counts on 5 Charges (signed 2/9/06). All of this after 60 days of me in limbo but "continuing investigation".

I submit that my counsel's attempt to meet with the Superintendent regarding my rights under Article 138 triggered a retaliatory action in the preparation of the ill founded charges against me that were signed on 9 February. I say ill founded because the Convening Authority saw fit to dismiss 10 of the 13 sex related offenses that were charged, following the recommendation of the Article 32 Investigating Officer. I submit that these charges were crafted to make me appear as a sexual predator and justify my continued separation from the Corps of Cadets and by invoking charges under the UCMJ, preclude me from exercising my rights to complain about the treatment I was receiving from my Commanding Officer. This action was in violation of the law and materially unfair.

By this action, I my banished status was continued such that even if I were to be found not guilty of every charge I face I was arbitrarily removed from academic training in December by the Commandant of Cadets and maintained in that status for the entire semester contrary to the provisions of the Academy Regulations. I would also submit that the Naval Academy was able to address these issues without imposing this punishment on the Midshipmen similarly accused of rape, which makes my circumstance appear arbitrary, capricious and an abuse of discretion.

On February 16, 2006 the Academy contacted the New London Day newspaper and advised them that I had been charged and a general overview of the charge substance which per further disseminated by the Associated Press and the television networks to the great embarrassment of my parents and public humiliation of both them and me. The Academy had avoided giving information to the media by stating that the matter was under investigation. I fail to see the meaningful distinction regarding public disclosure between pre-charge investigation and the UCMJ mandated Art 32 investigation. I believe that this action was directed by the Commandant of Cadets or at least with his approval. This was continuing mistreatment directed at me, particularly since 10 of those 16 specifications were dismissed.

The remaining charges and additional charges that have been referred to the GCM will be addressed in that arena but as stated above I feel that I have been wronged by my Commanding Officer as these circumstances have progressed.

/s/
Webster Smith 1/C

<u>There is no record of the disposition of this Article 138 Complaint.</u> If it had been disposed of with proper due process, it is doubtful if the General court-martial would have taken place.

A reliable and well placed source has informed me that the family of former cadet Webster Smith has been unable to get a copy of the disposition of the Article 138 Complaint.

CHAPTER 5

The Runaway Jury

The presumption of innocence is a principle that requires the government to prove the guilt of a criminal defendant and relieves the defendant of any burden to prove his or her innocence. It is essential to the criminal process. The mere mention of the phrase presumed innocent keeps judges and juries focused on the ultimate issue at hand in a criminal case: whether the prosecution has proven beyond a reasonable doubt that the defendant committed the alleged acts. The people of the United States have rejected the alternative to a presumption of innocence—a presumption of guilt—as being inquisitorial and contrary to the principles of a free society.

The Supreme Court has ruled that, under some circumstances, a court should issue jury instructions on the presumption of innocence in addition to instructions on the requirement of proof beyond a reasonable doubt. A presumption of innocence instruction may be required if the jury is in danger of convicting the defendant on the basis of extraneous considerations rather than the facts of the case. That is precisely what happened in the Webster Smith case.

In his opening statement to the Jury Panel on June 26, 2006 the prosecutor, Commander Ronald Bald, described Cadet Smith as a manipulative senior who preyed on lonely women.

Cadet Smith pleaded not guilty in the first court-martial of a cadet in Coast Guard Academy history. The charges ranged from rape, sodomy, and extortion to assault of the female cadets.

He was tried before a jury panel of Coast Guard officers including four white men, one white woman, three Black men and a man of Asian descent. The senior member was a captain with command experience. There were no cadets on the panel. Since there were no cadets on the jury panel, it can truly be asked whether he was afforded the best qualified jury or a jury of his peers. Were the best qualified members appointed to the panel, as the Manual For Courts-martial (MCM) and the UCMJ mandate?

The Uniform Code of Military Justice (UCMJ), (10 USC sec.801 et seq.) supplemented by the Manual For Courts-martial (MCM) provides guidance for a commander empowered to convene a court-martial. The UCMJ and the MCM both contain the following sentence:

"When convening a court-martial the convening authority shall detail as members thereof, such members of the armed forces as, in his opinion, are best qualified for the duty by reason of age, education, training, experience, length of service, and judicial temperament. (UCMJ Art. 25(d)(2)

The MCM specifically states that if it is anticipated that complicated issues of law will be presented before a special court-martial, the convening authority should give consideration to appointing as a member of the court a qualified attorney-at-law. In the Webster Smith case there were no complicated issues of law, but there were some complicated issues of fact. Such being the case, it would have been appropriate for the convening authority to detail at least one first class cadet to the jury panel. The failure to do so prejudiced the case against Webster Smith before the trial started.

In courts-martial constituted similar to the Smith court-martial, I have made the following or a similar argument many times while serving as defense counsel. None of the members of Webster Smith's jury panel had been a cadet at the USCGA while female cadets were living in Chase Hall. Only one had ever attended the USCGA; none had socialized with female cadets; none had attended cadet athletic parties; none had read the cadet regulations; none had counseled a cadet concerning sexual assault; none had first-hand experience with the four class system; none had indoctrinated female cadets; and none had ever had a cadet girl friend. In the unlikely event that any panel member had ever dated a female cadet, chances are that cadet would not have been the first female regimental commander, who got pregnant, had an abortion. A cadet who continued to date Webster Smith, the putative father, for another six months as a cadet while living in Chase Hall.

Only after being counseled by Coast Guard lawyers did she come to the conclusion that she might have a credible argument that she might have been raped at some point during her 18 month relationship with the accused. Added to all that was the female rumor mill in Chase Hall that was ringing with the news that Webster Smith was dating another female and he had told her about the Regimental Commander's pregnancy.

If, at least, one cadet had been on that jury, he could have explained to the members during deliberations many of the things that they were completely ignorant of. I contend that the jury did not have a clue as to what living conditions were like in Chase Hall, nor did they know what the social environment was like between Black male upper-class cadets and white female cadets in any of the four classes.

The members who sat on the Webster Smith jury panel probably did not know that cadets are in charge of the day to day affairs in Chase Hall. Cadets run the barracks. Officers are not normally permitted in Chase Hall without a cadet escort. So, many officers might not be aware of the atmosphere that prevails in Chase Hall. It would be difficult for one who has not lived in Chase Hall to put the testimony of a cadet about social happenings into proper perspective.

The cadets in Chase Hall speak a different language than the panel members were familiar with. Here are a few typical examples. In Chase Hall the roommate of a cadet is called his "wife". This was before women were admitted as cadets. An under-class cadet who runs errands for an upper-class cadet is called his "slave", dating back to the days of Hopley Yeaton, the Father of the Coast Guard. Every upper-class cadet has had, at least, two wives and a slave. Ordinary words are given different meanings in the cadet lexicon.

Without an upper-class cadet to resolve ambiguities and to explain simple terms, the members were forced to speculate, assume, and to read between the lines of the testimony that they heard. In all likelihood, they probably did not correctly interpret the testimony given by the cadets at the Webster Smith trial. Without a cadet on the jury panel, the convening authority did not detail the best qualified members in terms of age, experience, training, and judicial temperament. That being the case, the jury was not composed of the best qualified people available in accordance with the UCMJ and Art 25(d)(2).

Cadet Smith's attorneys raised the possibility that the charges could have been racially motivated. They said they were pleased by the

jury's diversity. Cadet Smith is a Black American, but all the accusers were white females.

Cadet Smith's Detailed Military Counsel, <u>LT Stuart Kirkby</u>, a Navy Judge Advocate General, compared the case to the Salem witch trials, in which people were put to death based on concocted stories that were not backed up by evidence.

With no physical evidence in the case, defense attorneys had hoped to persuade jurors that the testimony of the women was unreliable. There was no DNA evidence, no forensic evidence, no rape kit and no crime scene photos. It was a classic case of "he-said, she-said". It was one cadet's word against another. Any jury of reasonable men and women would have had a tough time trying to evaluate the credibility of one cadet against another, even though one was a Black man and the other was a white woman. However, the Convening Authority did something subtle but very shrewd. He waited until the white females had graduated from cadets to officers. That made a world of difference at the trial.

An officer is as far from a cadet as the East is from the West. It matters little that not more than 24 hours before the officers were themselves cadets. The perception of the jury was that of an officer making an accusation against a cadet. They saw female officers accusing a cadet; they did not see cadet classmates slandering each other. They did not see former lovers getting revenge and pay-back for betrayal of trust.

The defense counsel team, CDR Smith and LT Kirkby, failed to try to offset this psychological disadvantage. They let the female officers testify in uniform wearing all that gold. One after another, a parade of white female officers walked in and took the witness stand and lambasted the Black cadet. At the very least, all the witnesses should have been required to appear in civilian attire. A Roman Catholic priest would not have been allowed to testify wearing his clerical collar. It would have been highly prejudicial to the accused. It would have given the witness extra indicia of truth telling. It would enhance the credibility of the witness in the eyes of the jury, and perhaps even the judge. This is part of the psychology of trying a criminal case.

Cadet Webster Smith had lost the credibility battle before the jury panel retired to deliberate. <u>Webster Smith took the witness stand and testified at his own court-martial</u>. Normally, it is not a good idea to let the accused testify at his own trial. Cross-examination can be quite vigorous. He enjoys a Constitutional right to remain silent and not to incriminate himself. He is wrapped in a Constitutional presumption of innocence. The Government must prove its case beyond a reasonable doubt. Until that happens, the accused is presumed to be innocent.

The judge must instruct the jury that no adverse inference can be made from the fact that the accused did not testify. However, perhaps because there were so many female officers testifying against Cadet Smith, his Defense Attorneys may have felt that the volume of the evidence forced them to put their client on the witness stand.

One of the hardest decisions a defense attorney has to make is <u>whether to put his client on the witness stand</u>. I never allowed any of my clients to testify in their own behalf. I always had the distinct feeling that they would perjure themselves. The first thing they taught us in Law School was that your client always lies.

Webster Smith had two lawyers. It is not clear who made the decision to allow Webster Smith to take the Witness Stand. I believe it was a fatal error.

An independent military defense (DMC) counsel is detailed free of charge regardless of the accused's ability to pay. The accused may also employ civilian counsel (ICC) at his or her own expense, or request a particular military counsel (IMC), who will assist the accused if reasonably available. The accused has the right to be represented by counsel at the magistrate hearing when a determination is made regarding continued pretrial confinement, at the Article 32 investigation, and during all court-martial sessions. After trial, the accused has a right to free military counsel to assist with his appeal through the military appellate courts, and potentially to the U.S. Supreme Court.

The military assigned counsel is called the Detailed Military Counsel (DMC). The hired civilian counsel is called the Individual Military counsel (IMC). How Webster Smith ended up with a Navy Lawyer, is a real mystery. The Coast Guard had plenty of Law Specialists. Why was Webster Smith not assigned a Coast Guard Lawyer as his DMC? Equally as puzzling is why did two different lawyers in the Office of The Chief Counsel tell me that there was no court-martial of a Coast Guard Academy cadet taking place at the Academy? It was a simple question. I asked two lawyers during the work day at Coast Guard Headquarters, and they both denied any knowledge of a court-martial of a cadet at the Academy. I kept calling until I got an answer. I called a classmate of mine named Paul Ibsen. He was my classmate from the Academy Class of 1968 and was at the time working in the administration of some coeducational college preparatory school Charlotte, North Carolina. Yet, he was aware of the cadet court-martial at the CGA. It is unbelievable to me that two lawyers at Coast Guard Headquarters did not know this. I had to conclude that they were not telling me the truth. Why?

It is my opinion that no Coast Guard lawyer would take the case; and, it appears that the senior Assignment Officers in the Legal Office would not force anyone to take Webster Smith's case. Why, probably because it was a career destroyer. Anyone associated with the defense of Webster Smith would not survive as a Coast Guard Officer. This case was that hot. It was toxic. Anyone who came near it in the defense of Webster Smith would not get promoted. Yet, everyone associated with the Prosecution was promoted and rewarded. Commander Sean P. Gill was promoted and advanced to the Coast Guard Court of Criminal Appeals. The judges on the U.S. Coast Guard Court of Criminal Appeals at the end of fiscal year 2013 were:

Chief Judge Lane I. McClelland
Judge Patrick J. McGuire
Judge John F. Havranek

Judge Kathleen A. Duignan

Judge Andrew Norris

Judge Sean P. Gill (sworn in 8 May 2013)

Judge John S. Luce (sworn in 8 May 2013)

The Coast Guard has <u>one general court-martial judge</u> and six collateral-duty special court-martial judges. For the Webster Smith general Court-martial, the presiding judge was Captain Brian Judge. He is currently sitting as a member of The Coast Guard Court of Criminal Appeals. The Court is currently constituted as follows:

Chief Judge Lane I. McClelland

Judge John F. Havranek

Judge Kathleen A. Duignan

Judge Andrew J. Norris

Judge Peter J. Clemens

Judge Amy E. Kovac

Judge Benes Z. Aldana

Judge Laurina M. Spolidoro

Judge Robert W. Bruce

Judge Brian M. Judge

Who drafted <u>LT Stuart Kirkby as</u> the DMC? He was not a Coast Guard Law Specialist. He was a Navy Judge Advocate General from the Naval Submarine Base at Groton, Connecticut. <u>CDR Merle Smith</u>, USCG (Ret), had been a Coast Guard Law Specialist, and a part-time Law Professor at the Academy. He was hired by Cleon Smith to act as Cadet Smith's IMC.

The IMC is the Senior Attorney. He is sometimes called "The First Chair". He is senior to the DMC, who is called The Second Chair". The lawyers usually always fight among themselves before they fight the opposing counsels. I believe there was serious tension between the IMC and the DMC.

I faced similar situations when I was a retired Coast Guard Law Specialist representing Coast Guard members at Coast Guard Base New

York in courts-martial. However, I never had to assert my authority as lead counsel, Individual Military Counsel (IMC). The Coast Guard always detailed the most junior and inexperienced military counsel to the members that I represented. They were only qualified to carry my brief case and take notes, and they knew it. They were content to observe and listen and sometimes offer a helpful comment. I had just retired; I knew the Uniform Code of Military Justice; I knew the accused; and I knew the judges and all of the members of the Prosecution team; so, I was better qualified to represent the accused. And the military counsels knew this, so , they never challenged my decisions in conducting the defense of the accused.

There was serious tension between CDR Smith and LT Kirkby. LT Kirkby was very dissatisfied with the way CDR Smith was handling the Case. The tension and friction became so acute that it required several emergency sessions with the parents of Cadet Webster Smith to settle the issues. At one point, LT Kirkby told the parents, if you do not allow me to handle the cross-examination of this witness, your son will probably go to jail for a long time.

There were disagreements about who to put on the witness list, who to call as a witness, who would make the Opening Statement, who would make the Closing Argument, who would argue which motion, which motions to bring, who would examine which witnesses, who would make objections to statements and questions by the Prosecution, whether to give interviews to the news media, which questions to ask which witness; and , the biggest issue of all, whether to put the Accused, Webster Smith, on the witness stand. That is always a crucial decision. In the Webster Smith Case, it may have been the one issue that decided the final verdict in the case.

Having prosecuted and defended in many court-martials, I know that the average military jury member cares very little about the right of the accused to remain silent, or the right not to testify. They also pay little attention to the judge's instructions not to draw any adverse inferences from the fact that the accused refused to testify. Time after time following a courts-martial I have heard jury members say we wanted to hear what the accused had to say. They say that the accused should testify if he has nothing to hide. Also, they feel that the accused would not be on trial unless he had done something. He may not have committed the acts that he stood accused of, but he must have done something somewhere along the way. He finally had gotten caught. In this case with one female officer after another testifying against a cadet, it was virtually certain that the jury was going to find him guilty of something. The cards were stacked too high against him. In a case of pure "he-said, she-said", it would be a bit difficult to give the jury any portion of "he-said" without the accused taking the witness stand in his behalf. The rules prohibiting the admission of hearsay evidence forced the accused to take the stand.

Only in a court-martial tried by a "judge alone" can an accused be reasonably certain that no adverse inference would be drawn from his refusal to testify. Only then can an accused take a chance on relying upon his constitutionally guaranteed presumption of innocence.

If I had been the lead counsel in this case, I would have requested a trial before a judge alone. In which case, I would only have had to convince one person of the innocence of my client. Or to be precisely correct, I would have had only to convince one person that the Government had not sustained its burden of proof. That is to say, the prosecution had not proven my client was guilty beyond a reasonable doubt. Until that had occurred, my client was still presumed to be innocent. A jury is like a box of chocolate; you never know what you are going to get.

The burden of proof is not on the accused; it is on the prosecution. The burden never shifts. It is always on the Government. The accused is not required to prove his innocence. That is his constitutional guarantee. He is presumed to be innocent.

Commander Ronald Bald, the prosecutor argued that Webster Smith's stories do not make sense and that the defense did not prove that his accusers concocted their stories in a conspiracy against him. That was totally improper and objectionable. He was arguing to the jury that

Webster Smith was required to prove his innocence or they should convict him.

The Prosecutor went on to argue to the jury that "The defense hasn't given you a sisterhood. They haven't given you a conspiracy. They haven't given you collusion". This would clearly appear to be prosecutorial misconduct and should have been reversible error. I cannot imagine any instruction from the military judge that would have cured the harm done by such an argument.

That argument alone set the Anglo-American judicial system back more than 200 years. It took American justice back to a time before we had drafted a Constitution, or fashioned a presumption of innocence, or afforded an accused a right not to incriminate himself and to remain silent. It is inconceivable that this mockery of a trial took place in an American court in 2006.

If the defense had tried this case before a judge alone, and if Webster Smith had not testified, based on the testimony adduced at trial, it would have been virtually impossible for the Government to prove its case based on the testimony of SR alone. There was no physical evidence. The case was based on the credibility of the witnesses. If Webster Smith had not put his credibility in issue by taking the witness stand, it is my concerted opinion that the judge would have had to dismiss the charges at the end of the Defense's case in chief. It is at that point in a trial that the defense usually makes a motion to dismiss the charges because the Government had not proven all of the elements of the offenses beyond a reasonable doubt.

Moreover, in a trial before a judge alone, I would never have allowed my client to get anywhere near the witness stand. I would have rested my case without calling any witnesses. I would have taken the chance that the judge's oath as a judicial officer to weigh the evidence objectively and fairly would out-weigh his possible human prejudices as a white man.

One may argue that this is Monday morning quarterbacking at its worst. However, now that all of the relevant facts are on the table, it is clear that the Government really had no case. It was counting on Webster Smith to lose the case. That would be like a husband losing an uncontested divorce case. This would explain why the Article 32 Investigating Officer recommended to the Convening Authority that he should not convene a court-martial. The minor charges, like disobeying an order not to try to contact any of his classmates, could have been dealt with at an Article 15 Captain's Mast. That would have constituted non-judicial punishment.

On June 28, 2006 after about eight hours of deliberation, the panel found Cadet Webster Smith guilty of indecent assault, extortion in exchange for sexual favors and sodomy, which in military parlance includes oral sex. All those charges involved only one of the four accusers, SR. He was acquitted of several charges that stemmed from alleged sexual encounters with the other three female cadets. The defense had argued that the sex was consensual and that the women had colluded against Webster Smith. They were all scorned lovers of one sort or another. Hell has no fury like a woman scorned. With no physical evidence outside of e-mails and phone records, the trial pitted Smith's version of events against those of his accusers.

Smith was acquitted of all charges involving his conduct with all of the women, except SR. One, his former girlfriend (KN), testified that he raped her after she became intoxicated during a party at the Naval Academy in Annapolis, Maryland. She did not tell them that after she became pregnant and decided to get an abortion, it was Webster Smith who took her to the hospital. He also took care of her and ran errands for her while she convalesced after the abortion. Then he kept their secret for over six months. When he made the fatal mistake of divulging their secret she turned against him.

Smith was found not guilty of the charge that started the investigation. In the course of the investigation information was uncovered that gave rise to other charges. He was found guilty of offenses found during the course of the investigation. He was sentenced to, among other things, six months in jail.

Of the 10 charges referred to the general court martial, Smith was acquitted of one charge of rape, one count of extortion, one count of sodomy, one count of indecent assault and one charge of assault (five of 10 charges). **All findings of guilty cited in the article related to one woman (SR)**. He was also convicted of two other minor military offenses. One was disobeying an order not to contact any other cadet directly or indirectly. He did not contact anyone, but he attempted to contact a friend. Moreover, his attempt to contact the friend took place the day before the order was issued.

The specification charged violation of a paragraph of a written order issued by the Commandant of Cadets on 7 December 2005. The Commandant of Cadets issued the written order of 5 December at the time Cadet Smith was removed from the barracks. Appellant to Coast

The order of 7 December alleged to have been violated read, "You are prohibited from any contact of any kind, directly or indirectly, through any source, or by any means, with Coast Guard Academy Cadets wherever they are located; to include text messages, emails, or phone calls." This differs from the order of 5 December by the added words, "directly or indirectly, though any source, or by any means," and "wherever they are located."

The specification alleged violation of the order by, "on or about 16 December 2005, … wrongfully sending an instant message to [KS], with the intention of having [KS] contact Cadet [KN]." KS and KN were close friends.

At Trial, Smith testified that he had sent an instant message to KS on 6 December 2005, before receiving information that he was not supposed to contact any cadets indirectly, but none after receiving the order the next day prohibiting indirect contact with KN.

Cadet Smith's attorney argued that his testimony was certain as to the date he sent the message and KS's testimony was uncertain, and therefore his version must be accepted. Apparently the members did not believe Smith's version and believed KS's testimony that she had received the instant message a few (less than ten) days before 16 December. The Court was satisfied that the evidence supported the finding that Smith sent the instant message after he received the 7 December order.

What the Court did not know was that KN had been communicating with Cadet Smith consistently through his mother and sister. I am sure that the witnesses had been instructed not to communicate with the Defendant, Cadet Smith. Also, they were instructed not to discuss their testimony among themselves or with anyone. Those Instructions were completely ignored. Their violations were much more flagrant than the one attempt by Cadet Smith to contact KN. He went to jail for his violation. They just went on about their business. The Court was completely in different and in the dark.

A complete set of Emails from KN and KS sent to Cadet Smith indirectly through his mother and sister was turned over to the Defense Attorneys. They either did not offer them into evidence or the Judge refused to accept them. Well, those Emails are available here. They are presented in Appendix 9.

However, that is not the full story. The incidents related to Cadet Smith were publicly announced as 16 pending charges in mid-February 2006. These charges related to five women. In early 2006 the Coast Guard Investigative Service (CGIS) undertook an investigation related to yet another woman and Cadet Smith. This resulted in six additional charges, filed in March 2006. The Article 32 Investigation resulted in dismissal of 12 of the 22 charges. This is, **17 of 22 charged allegations were not substantiated (12 dismissals; five acquittals)**.

After spending about six months at hard labor and pre-trial confinement, Cadet Smith was sentenced to an additional six months in jail at a Navy brig. No credit was given for the time already served in confinement. In a normal case like this, the six months of pre-trial confinement would have been credited to the sentence adjudged. The accused would not have had to serve any additional time in confinement. About forty years after Merle James Smith became the first Black American to enter the Coast Guard Academy in 1962, Webster Smith had become the first cadet to be tried by court-martial and sent to jail in 2006. The first female cadets entered in 1976, and they were making enormous strides. Vice Admiral Manson K. Brown, Class of 1978, had been the first Black Regimental Commander. LT Kristen Nicolson, Class of 2006, was the first female Regimental Commander.

Adding female cadets to the cadet barracks at Chase Hall had certainly changed the chemistry within the corps of cadets. Living side by side in the cadet barracks introduced new challenges to the strict military discipline required by the UCMJ, cadet regulations, and the Honor Concept.

Athletic celebrations on and off campus took on a new dimension. Binge drinking and illegal drugs became a staple. Women gave as good as they got. Sexual encounters of every description became common. How many women became pregnant and had abortions we will never know. There was one that we are positive of. She was Webster Smith's girlfriend.

All of the female cadets involved with and associated with Webster Smith escaped clean without any consequences for their actions or their behavior. Mother Nature was the only one who exacted a penalty. Natural Law resulted in a pregnancy. An abortion followed. If women are equal, they should be treated as equal. Not a single woman was disciplined under the UCMJ or the cadet regulations. All of the female cadets involved in this case graduated and were commissioned as

Coast Guard officers. Their testimony at the court-martial painted a picture of female cadets who were untrustworthy, arrogant, and certainly not ladies. **Their conduct was unbecoming an officer and a lady.**

There were many bad decisions made in the course of convening this court-martial. The most regrettable is that it was deemed necessary. Another is that a message has been sent to all future cadets that women have the freedom to act as recklessly as men, yet at the same time they will be immune from consequences. How can women ever earn the complete respect of their male counterparts when they continually rely upon their gender trump card? They are forever destined to be daddy's girl; always cream puffs with almost the right stuff. This case has shown every cadet that women can get the same privileges as men and not have to shoulder the same responsibilities. The Coast Guard applied a double standard with respect to gender, and a discriminatory standard with respect to race and ethnic origin.

The <u>Witnesses for the Prosecution</u> were; Shannon Frobel (SF), Stacy Chmieleski (SC), Keri McCormack (KM), Natalie Moyer (NM), Shelly Rodenbush (SR), Kristin Strizki (KS), and Kristen Nicholson (KN)). All of the witnesses were Coast Guard Academy Cadets except KS. Midshipman Kristin Strizki, was a midshipman at the U. S. Naval Academy. She was the final witnesses for the government at the Article 32 Investigative Hearing on March 21, 2006.

There was one other name on The List, **(Katie Collela)** but she was able to get her father to persuade CDR Gill and CAPT Wisniewski to take her name off The List. For one thing, she really liked Webster Smith. She had dated him; she had invited him over to the house for Christmas Dinner. She even drove to the Academy to pick him up. Also, both her parents were senior Coast Guard officers. Moreover, her father and Doug Wisniewski have known each other since the Academy.

These women were witnesses at a public trial yet they were accorded the equivalent of rape shield protection. This was not a rape case. Not one of the women had been raped. There was testimony of consensual sex acts. Some of the consensual sex acts were unlawful because, among other things, they occurred in Chase Hall, or at Academy functions. How could unlawful consensual sex acts result in charges against only one of the participants? It takes two to tango. What does it mean for a cadet or a future U.S. military officer to act like a lady? If Webster M. Smith is no gentleman and is unfit to be an officer in the U.S. Coast Guard, then so are the women he was involved with. These women are not ladies and are unfit to be commissioned officers. The women in this case should be held accountable to the same standard of conduct.

For a pure ice-water jolt to the senses few juries in recent years have surprised me as much as the Webster Smith court-martial jury. The verdict is in on the jury. We know that, at least, seven of the nine members were brain-dead. One was certifiably insane. This jury said, in essence, we are not concerned about the truth. We can't handle the truth. Just give us enough facts to buttress our predispositions. We can't be bothered with such legal niceties as who has the burden of proof, or whether he has met that burden, or whether all the elements of the offense have been proved beyond a reasonable doubt. Cadet Smith has not proven to us that he did not do it. If he was not guilty of something, then they would not have convened this General Court-martial. We are ready to convict based on the prosecution's theory of the case. Pure conjecture, rank supposition, and casual coincidence are enough for us.

It is truly shocking to the conscience how far this jury was prepared to go to ignore the evidence and to send a message to the fleet. You could get <u>more justice from a firing squad</u> than the president of this jury was prepared to give this poor cadet.

Anyone who has not seen "Twelve Angry Men" should run out and buy it. After you have watched it you will have some sense of what the deliberations were like in the Webster Smith case. There was a four-bagger in there, that is a Coast Guard Captain, arguing for 5 years of confinement and a $100,000.00 fine; and a two-stripper, that is a Lieutenant, pleading for no more than 6 months of confinement. Thankfully this junior officer had the courage of his convictions. After hours of haggling, the jury only awarded 6 months confinement.

The Lieutenant wanted the punishment to fit the crime, but the senior officer wanted to send a message to the fleet that this is how the Coast Guard handles sexual predators. How sad. He sent a message alright. The message was heard loud and clear around the world. The message was that wisdom does not come with age, nor does sound judgment come with rank. The message was that a General Court-martial jury panel was prepared to destroy Cadet Webster Smith and bankrupt his family purely on the disputed and uncorroborated testimony of a coached witness.

It is shocking that some senior officers can exercise such poor judgment. In their reckless rush to send a message to the fleet that this is how the Coast Guard handles sexual predators, they did not want to be confused with the truth that Webster Smith was set-up. Some of the jurors were prepared to sacrifice Mrs. Smith's pride and joy to make a statement. This was to be another first for the Coast Guard. Not content merely to be the first service academy to admit women, these officers wanted the Coast Guard Academy to be the first to show the world how the Coast Guard will legally and with due process make an example of an innocent cadet. A mind is a terrible thing to waste, but they wanted to waste the life of Webster Smith to make a point.

The world was not the only ones watching. The corps of cadets was also going to school on what was happening in Hamilton Hall. This was the Doug Wisniewski School of Ethics, and Judgment 101. His concept of military justice more resembles ritual sacrifice. The cadets in Chase Hall saw senior officers recklessly out of control. They saw Captain Doug Wisniewski cannibalizing the cadet corps. Honor was dead. The Honor Code and the Honor Concept were observed more in the breach than at all. Keep your head down and say nothing. All of a sudden it is dog eat dog and every man for himself. In a rat race only the biggest rat can win. Long live King Rat. This is the Legacy of Doug Wisniewski.

Cadet Smith's Legal Dream Team, CDR Smith and LT Kirkby, raised the possibility that the charges could have been racially motivated. They said they were pleased by the jury's diversity. Cadet Smith is a Black American, but all the accusers were white females. With no physical evidence in the case, defense attorneys had hoped to persuade jurors that the testimony of the women was unreliable. There was no DNA evidence, no forensic evidence, no rape kit and no crime scene photos. It was a classic case of "he-said, she-said". It was one cadet's word against another.

Any jury of reasonable men and women would have had a tough time trying to evaluate the credibility of one cadet against another, even though one was a Black man and the other was a white woman. However, the Convening Authority did something subtle but very shrewd. He waited until the white females had graduated from cadet to officer. That made a world of difference at the trial. An officer is as far from a cadet as the East is from the West. It matters little that not more than 24 hours before the officer was herself a cadet. The perception of the jury was that of an officer making an accusation against a cadet. They saw female officers accusing a cadet; they did not see cadet classmates slandering each other. They did not see former lovers getting revenge and pay-back for betrayal of trust.

Webster Smith appealed his conviction all the way to the Supreme Court. The U.S. Coast Guard Court of Criminal Appeals scheduled oral arguments in the Case of The Appeal of the Court-martial Conviction of Cadet Webster Smith for January 16, 2008 in Arlington, Virginia. A legal brief filed by his lawyers claimed the convictions should be thrown out because the defense team was not allowed to fully cross-examine one of his accusers during Smith's court martial. They said that meant the jury didn't hear testimony that the accuser, a female cadet, (SR), had once had consensual sex with a Coast Guard enlisted man and then called it sexual assault.

LCDR Patrick M. Flynn, the government's lawyer for the Coast Guard Court of Criminal Appeals, said 27 November 2008 that the jury "heard enough" and the trial judge was within his rights to impose reasonable limits on the cross-examination.

"They didn't need to hear the additional details the defense is arguing they should have been allowed to hear." The defense also was asking the court to set aside Smith's convictions on two lesser charges of failing to obey an order and abandoning watch.

CHAPTER 6

Go Straight To Jail

A kangaroo court is a proceeding that denies proper procedure in the name of expediency. It is a fraudulent or unjust trial where the decision has essentially been made in advance, usually for the purpose of providing a conviction. It is also an elaborately scripted event intended to appear fair while having the outcome predetermined from the start. It is a show trial with a reasonable outcome.

As in the case of Webster Smith, it is conducted largely in the open. An accounting of private conduct is done in public. The proceedings appear to be fair, and the sentence is apparently legitimate. The convening authority goes out of its way to be open and fair, but it is nothing more than a show trial. It results in a judicial lynching; such as, Stalin's kangaroo trials of his "enemies", and the Romanian military court which sentenced Nicolae Ceausescu to death.

Associate Justice of the Supreme Court WILLIAM O. DOUGLAS once wrote, "[W]here police take matters in their own hands, seize victims, beat and pound them until they confess, there cannot be the slightest doubt that the police have deprived the victim of a right under the Constitution. **It is the right of the accused to be tried** by a legally constituted court, **not by a kangaroo court**" (*Williams v. United States*, 341 U.S. 97, 71 S. Ct. 576, 95 L. Ed. 774 [1951]).

After his kangaroo court-martial, former Cadet Webster Smith was taken to the U.S. Navy brig at the Submarine Base in Groton, Connecticut on 28 June 2006. He should have been granted an 8 day deferment of the sentence. This is normally a routine thing. However, this was not a routine case, by any means. Even the vilest military convicted offender is given some time alone with his family to say good-bye. Webster Smith was not. Webster waited in a secure room under double security guards while his written Request for Deferment was presented to Admiral James Van Sice. The Admiral sat in his ivory tower with Commander Sean Gill, his military advisor, and drank coffee. Then he summarily denied the routine request without any justification whatsoever. This has never been done before. Admiral Van Sice received bad advice from his legal advisor.

As soon as Van Sice's signature was on the denial order, two flat-footed agents from the Coast Guard Investigative Service (CGIS) ordered Cadet Smith's parents to vacate the premises. Mild mannered Webster Smith was handcuffed and paraded up and down the corridor like Jesus being paraded between Caiaphas and Pontius Pilate for all the rabble to gawk and marvel. Poor Webster Smith was made a spectacle. Thoroughly humbled and suitably constrained, he was offered for inspection to KN and SR, the two principal witnesses against him. Then, still in handcuffs, he was paraded in front of the news media for a photo opportunity. This was cruel and inhuman punishment. This was truly a new low even for the likes of James Van Sice. This single act more so than preferring groundless charges shows clearly the character of

Admiral James Van Sice. His actions indicated that he was not only a racist, and a bigot, but he was also just plain mean spirited.

Originally he was supposed to be transferred on 10 July to a Federal prison for military officers in South Carolina. It did not happen. Admiral Van Sice delayed signing off on the Report of the Court-martial. The delay was not explained. Then plans were to transfer him to the South Carolina prison on 19 July. Commandant Instruction M5350.4B, The Civil Rights Manual, required the Academy Civil Rights Officer to attempt to resolve informally any civil rights complaint within 5 days of receiving it. Jo Ann Miller, the Academy Civil Rights Officer, planned to retire on 28 July.

To expect this travesty of justice to have a positive effect upon the Coast Guard Academy is tantamount to asking for good fruit to come from a poisonous tree. It will not happen. It will not result in gender equality. It will not make female cadets take responsibility for their own actions. It will not result in more female staff officers at the Academy. Having a female Commandant of Cadets is nice but it is little more than window dressing. It will not turn female coeds at a secular college into female cadets or future Coast Guard officers. It will not cause the Coast Guard to change its policy on releasing the statistics they keep on the number of reported sexual assaults on base.

All of the other military academies have released their statistics on sexual assaults reported. The public has access to those statistics. The Coast Guard has not released the number of assaults reported, or how they were disposed of. There have been many, up to and during the time Webster Smith was in pre-trial confinement. All of the others have been quietly disposed of. From 1993 until the spring semester of 2005, the Coast Guard had confirmed only 10 reported incidents of sexual misconduct, according to information provided by the Coast Guard Academy to the Navy Times. Of those, six incidents resulted in dismissal of the accused and two ended in resignation. In the remaining two cases, there was insufficient evidence to pursue charges. The Coast

Guard Academy had 982 students, nearly 30 percent of whom were women at that time.

Only Webster Smith has been persecuted and then prosecuted to the fullest extent possible under the Uniform Code of Military Justice. So far, we have only heard of the most exceptional cases that get reported in the media. The Coast Guard guards its sexual assault statics like the nuclear missile launch codes. It is arguable whether they would release the statistics pursuant to a Freedom of Information Act Request (FOIA). Of course, they would be subject to a subpoena as part of discovery in a discrimination law suit. Or the NAACP Legal Defense, Inc Fund or the Department of Justice could just ask for them. Now that U.S. Representative Rosa DeLauro, D-Conn., has proposed a federal review of the Coast Guard Academy's sexual assault policies and the Government Accounting Office (GAO) is taking closer cognizance of the Coast Guard Academy, I am sure that they will keep a close eye on the statistics.

CHAPTER 7

The Man Who Perverted Justice At The USCGA

The Case of Webster Smith spawned investigations, a task force, and the Case of Admiral James Van Sice. The Case of Admiral James Van Sice could have proven to be a most unusual case. It would have been unusual because he could have been charged with **crimes committed in the name of the Law**; that is to say, the Legal PROCESS. Admiral Van Sice and Captain Douglas Wisniewski definitely misused the Legal PROCESS.

This is all the more ironic because these men were the embodiment of what passed for Justice, integrity, and authority at the Coast Guard Academy (CGA). A Task Force appointed by the Commandant, Admiral Thad Allen, and a Special Investigating Flag Officer in the 5th Coast Guard District investigated Admiral Van Sice. This was altogether fitting and proper. This was just as it should have been, because only another Flag Officer, such as an admiral, could know the level of trust and the awesome amount of power that is bestowed upon a man in that position. Only another officer with that many **years of experience who had convened courts-martial could know** how much more a court-martial is than just a panel of officers sitting in judgment on a cadet, or how much more a court is than simply a court room.

It is **a PROCESS**; it is **a spirit**. It is the Palace of Justice. It is where men expect to be judged fairly because true Justice is blind.

These men **distorted** and **perverted** justice at the Coast Guard Academy. They **hijacked** the legal PROCESS. They used the military justice system as an instrument of their **personal vengeance**. When they sailed into uncharted waters and convened a court-martial to try a cadet, they torpedoed Justice and shattered the illusion of fairness at the Academy. This was a horrendous crime against humanity. This was nothing less than dereliction of duty and malfeasance in office. This was a conscious betrayal of the oath that they took to defend and to protect the Constitution of the United States against all enemies, both foreign and domestic.

Van Sice and Wisniewski are, themselves, Coast Guard Academy graduates. Between them they have almost 60 years of experience as Coast Guard officers. They reached maturity over 2 generations ago. They are well educated adults in positions of public trust. They, most of all, should have valued **Justice, Honor, Truth, and Fairness.** They should have been capable of being entrusted with the responsibility for the administration of the PROCESS.

The United States and much of the world watched and waited to see what would be the outcome of this case. This was truly a case without precedent. It is a case that will live in infamy.

Justice was ravished by Admiral Van Sice. We have to re-consecrate the Temple of Justice at the Academy and in the entire U. S. Coast Guard. The entire Coast Guard was placed on trial when cadet Webster Smith was charged. The character of every Coast Guard officer and Academy graduate was placed in issue when the Academy Superintendent accused a man of raping his girlfriend 6 months after she had aborted their child and continued a meaningful relationship with him.

Webster Smith was at the beginning of a process that had produced Van Sice and Wisniewski. They were at opposite ends of the pipe line that turns out Commissioned Coast Guard officers. So, the goals and the accomplishments of the Academy were called into question when the two most senior officers at the Academy chose to court-martial a cadet. Even more so, when they chose to ignore the advice of the law specialist they detailed to investigate the charges. That was the Article 32 Investigating Officer who reported to them that the facts would not sustain a conviction for rape. They chose to accept the advice of the Academy staff legal officer over that of the Article 32 Investigating Officer.

A General Court-martial was not necessary to get an accused sent to jail for 6 months. A Special Court-martial could have done that. **This was over-kill**. Even a Summary Court-martial would have been able to send Webster Smith to jail for 30 days. One has to ask what was it that drove these two senior, experienced officers almost mad; so mad, in fact, that they placed their own careers in jeopardy to punish a cadet. Was it the fact that Webster Smith's girlfriend was the first female Regimental Commander in over 7 years? Or, was it the fact that Doug Wisniewski had handpicked her? Was he secretly in love with her, and had he picked her for Regimental Commander to curry favor with her? Was the fact that she became pregnant by a Black man the ultimate act of infidelity and betrayal to him? Was that why he ordered Webster Smith out of the barracks at Chase Hall to prevent him from being able to talk to her? Was that why he placed him under a restraining order and forced him to work on the boat docks at hard labor many months before a charge sheet was even drafted or a court-martial was even convened?

The Webster Smith case gave the world a microscope to see into the character of these senior Coast Guard officers. It gave all of us a chance to look into the character and the values of the men who are charged with the security of the American Homeland. The Coast Guard is the lead agency in the Department of Homeland Security. Are these officers capable of sound judgment? Or do they betray the public trust; or take appropriated funds and buy beer brewing equipment or bar-b-que pits and party while people are suffering?

The big question is HOW! A good start would be to conduct a thorough honest investigation and evaluation of the culture and climate at the Academy. A Task Force has rendered its findings. Regrettably, it did not give a critique of the actions and judgments of all those responsible for the Webster Smith fiasco. The reinstatement of former Cadet Webster Smith and the expunging of his record would have been a good start.

Webster Smith has moved on with his life. He is married and has a child. However, he has bad paper that will follow him for the rest of his life. He must register as a sex offender in the State of Texas. A grant of clemency and a Presidential Pardon would be a giant step towards remedying the wrong that has been done.

However, that will not be enough. The **re-consecration of Justice at the Academy** will not be found in a Task Force Report. It will not be found in the Uniform Code of Military Justice, or in the Academy cadet regulations, or in any written documents that no one fully understands or denies. It will have to be found in **the character of the officers and cadets** in the Coast Guard and at the Coast Guard Academy.

CHAPTER 8

Who Played The Race Card In The Webster Smith Case?

Who played the race card in the Webster Smith case? Was it Commandant of Cadets Doug Wisniewski and CWO2 David French? Or was it Webster Smith's defense team? Could it have been the news media? Someone certainly did, because the race of the accused was reported before the trial began.

Excerpts from The Day newspaper said as follows: Defense lawyers say race is a factor in the case. Smith is black, his accusers are white, and defense attorneys suspect the women conspired to bring false accusations against him. If race wasn't a factor when six women accused Smith of sexual misconduct, Merle Smith said, it might have been when a seventh woman came forward and the academy added new charges. Most of the sex-related charges have been dismissed.

"...as this thing has continued to evolve, I guess, as the first 16 charges didn't appear to be going well, I guess they had to find another eight to see if they could make that case," Merle Smith said.

Academy officials have said they will not comment on specific allegations before the trial.

The jury of Coast Guard officers included four white men, one white woman, three black men and a man of Asian descent.

Admiral Allen is correct. In his State of the Coast Guard address he said, "We have never been more relevant and we have never been more visible to the Nation we serve".

We are more visible because we have received more publicity. For some people craving recognition, all publicity is good. It is free advertising. Not for an old and venerated service. For an old public service, bad publicity can be dangerous and disastrous.
There was security in our obscurity. Publicity is a blessing and a curse. You can no longer be hidden and presumed to be ethical, and competent. Now you have to demonstrate that competence, and you have to demonstrate the high moral behavior that you claim to have and want to instill in those coming after you. You cannot just talk that talk; now, you have to walk that walk.

The Smith case is the first court-martial of a cadet in the Academy's history. The Smith case brought a lot of sudden attention. The end of Van Sice's military career is more difficult news for the Academy. It has experienced a series of cadet run-ins with the law. The first and most prominent incident happened under Van Sice's watch. He is the father of the Webster Smith debacle. The Commandant of the Coast Guard would have gone a long way toward restoring public faith in the Coast Guard and in the Academy, if he had punished Admiral Van Sice more appropriately and if he had been more forthcoming with the details of his misconduct and the type of punishment.

Smith's attorneys, who raised the possibility that the charges could be racially motivated, said they were pleased by the jury's diversity. Smith is Black and the accusers are white.

In a January 21, 2006 article in The Day newspaper it was reported that from 1993 until the spring semester of 2005, the Coast Guard had 10 reported incidents of sexual misconduct, according to information provided by the academy. Of those, six incidents resulted in dismissal of the accused and two ended in resignation. In the remaining two cases, there was insufficient evidence to pursue charges.

One of the other two complaints, stemming from the first semester of 2005-06, resulted in a confession and the Dec. 15 dismissal of a first-year male student, who departed immediately, according to Chief Warrant Officer (CWO) French. He stated that a female cadet reported nonconsensual sexual advances from a freshman male in the Chase Hall barracks, the dormitory where all students reside.

No criminal charges were filed, French said. (Notice he said nonconsensual sexual advances. Is this what CWO French calls rape, when it is done by a white cadet?) It is safe to assume that none of the male cadets involved were African American, because whenever a Black male is involved the news report very explicitly points out that the male was Black, as was reported in the Webster Smith case. Smith, a linebacker on the academy's football team, was charged Feb. 9 under military law with rape, assault, indecent assault and sodomy against female cadets, said CWO David French, an academy spokesman.

The Associated Press reported on February 25, 2006 that a cadet was kicked out instead of prosecuted. (Note 3) A prosecutor said he was reviewing how information is exchanged with the U.S. Coast Guard Academy after learning a cadet who admitted sexual misconduct wasn't prosecuted but kicked out of school last year.

New London State's Attorney Kevin Kane would not say whether he believes he has jurisdiction in the case. An Academy spokesman said he could not comment on the case, citing privacy rules. "It was fully investigated and handled appropriately," Chief Warrant Officer David French said.

According to an Academy discipline summary, the male cadet was expelled in December after admitting to sexual misconduct that was determined to be nonconsensual. So, there were 10 reported cases from 1993 to 2005, and not one resulted in a court-martial. The first report of sexual misconduct involving a Black cadet resulted in a General court-martial. It was not just any court-martial, but the type reserved for murder, treason, and assault with intent to commit grievous bodily harm. The Coast Guard Academy had 982 students, nearly 30 percent of whom were women. If a report involving sexual assault or misconduct is made to the chain of command, CGIS must examine it. "The Commandant of Cadets, CAPT Douglas Wisniewski, took immediate action to initiate the investigation into these allegations", CWO2 David French said. French declined a request for an interview with Commandant of Cadets Capt. Douglas Wisniewski. The Coast Guard Academy largely limited its responses to brief written statements delivered by e-mail.

Captain Doug Wisniewski, who graduated from the academy with the last all-male class, was replaced by the first woman to hold the post, Captain Judith Keene, who graduated in the second class to accept women.

"Sexual misconduct at the academy is defined as "acts that disgrace or bring discredit on the Coast Guard or Coast Guard Academy and are sexual in nature", including lewd or lascivious acts, indecent exposure or homosexual conduct. But the definition also includes consensual acts that are prohibited on academy grounds, such as holding hands, kissing in public or sex. This does not include rape, because rape is not a consensual act. If the Academy disposes of 10 cases of sexual misconduct without a court-martial, but on the 11th case of a report of sexual misconduct it convenes a General court-martial, is that playing the race card? What if all 10 of the first cases involved only white cadets, but the 11th case involved a Black cadet? One has to ask why the Black cadet was singled out for a court-martial.

In the beginning there was the crime of sexual assault at the Coast Guard Academy, and the crime was white on white in Chase Hall. Then darkness moved upon the soul of Douglas Wisniewski, and Doug wanted to paint the face of the crime black. In those days there came a young, charismatic, and well liked cadet named Webster Smith, a cadet greatly favored by the coaching staff and the fairer sex. Webster Smith was a dreamer and he was black. Come now, said Captain Doug, let us

85

slay this dreamer and we will see what happens to his dream of being a Coast Guard officer. So, Wisniewski court-martialed Webster Smith and all the world wondered why.

Is it wrong for Black people to ask if there is a double standard? Would that amount to paranoia on the part of Black people? Or would that be considered playing the race card simply to inquire? Is it absurd to believe that anything more than pure chance resulted in the court-martial of Webster Smith? The fact that he was court-martialed speaks to a social reality that African-Americans are acutely aware of in America. Race is not a card to be dealt, but it determines whom the dealer is and who gets dealt a losing hand. In this case Doug Wisniewski dealt the cards, and he dealt from the bottom of the deck.

Whites are generally reluctant to acknowledge racism, but they are quick to accuse Black people of playing the race card. The tendency for whites to deny the extent of racism and racial injustice is reflected in the opinions solicited in Norwich on the day that Webster Smith was found guilty and later sentenced to six months in the brig. White comments were generally that this was a reasonable conclusion to the entire sorry affair. An Academy employee said that this is good. It shows that the Academy took timely and effective action. This was evidence of white denial and total indifference to Black persecution.

Unbelievably, Admiral Van Sice went out of his way to talk to Belinda Smith, Webster Smith's mother, during the trial. He kept assuring her that everything was going to be alright. He said "it will take some time, but as soon as the trial is over, everything is going to be alright". For whom? Was Admiral Van Sice in denial or did he think that Belinda and Cadet Webster Smith were expendable?

Perhaps this is why, contrary to popular belief, research indicates that people of color are actually reluctant to allege racism, be it on the job, or in schools, or anywhere else. Far from playing the race card at the drop of a hat, it is actually the case that black and brown folks typically stuff their experiences with discrimination and racism, only making an allegation of such treatment after many, many incidents have transpired, about which they said nothing for fear of being ignored or attacked.

So says Tim Wise, activist, lecturer and director of the new **Association for White Anti-Racist Education (AWARE).** Tim Wise works from anecdote rather than academic argument to recount his path to greater cultural awareness in a colloquial, matter-of-fact quasi-memoir that urges white people to fight racism 'for our own sake.' Wise is the author of two new books: **White Like Me: Reflections on Race from a Privileged Son** (Soft Skull Press, 2005), and **Affirmative Action: Racial Preference in Black and White**. In White Like Me, Wise offers a highly personal examination of the ways in which racial privilege shapes the lives of most white Americans, overtly racist or not, to the detriment of people of color, themselves, and society.

Precisely because white denial has long trumped claims of racism, people of color tend to underreport their experiences with racial bias, rather than exaggerate them. When it comes to playing the race card, it is more accurate to say that whites are the dealers with the loaded decks.

CHAPTER 9

CAN A WOMAN BE A SEXUAL PREDATOR?

Can a woman be a sexual predator? Who Was The Real Sexual Predator in The USCGA Class of 2006? Was it **Webster Smith** or **Shelly Roddenbush?** Who fraternized with enlisted members? Who had consensual sex with an enlisted member from another branch of the military and later lied about it? Whose conduct was more to the prejudice of good order and discipline?

Consider the case of Kelly Flinn. 1st Lieutenant **Kelly Flinn** faced a court-martial on May 20, 1997 for military charges of adultery with a civilian soccer coach at Minot Air Force Base who was married to a female enlisted subordinate; conduct unbecoming an officer; disobeying a lawful order (in writing, to stay away from the married man), and for making a false official statement. She attended the Air Force Academy and bomber training, becoming the first woman B-52 pilot in the USAF. Flinn's case, due to her high visibility in Air Force recruitment advertisements, as well as the number of her accomplishments during her four years of active-duty service, drew national attention, eventually creating a media circus culminating when the Chief of Staff of the Air Force General Ronald Fogleman made comments on her case at a congressional hearing. Following General Fogleman's comments, Lieutenant Flinn was allowed to resign from the Air Force by Secretary of the Air Force Dr. Sheila E. Widnall with a general discharge instead of facing a court-martial.

Flinn was the first female B-52 pilot in the USAF.Flinn was discharged from the U.S. Air Force in 1997 after being charged with making a false statement, adultery, and disobeying orders. Flinn's trouble with the Air Force received widespread media attention at the time and was discussed in a U.S. Senate hearing on May 22, 1997.

She later wrote a book recounting her experiences entitled Proud to Be: My Life, The Air Force, The Controversy. It has always been a consistent policy of the Air Force to prohibit and discourage relationships between officers and enlisted. While the media insists that she is being "unfairly singled out for adultery" (which is also prohibited under the UCMJ) in fact, what Lt. Flinn is charged with is disobeying a direct and legal order, and lying. It just happens that what **she was lying about was her adultery. She admits guilt to both charges**. She was deposed by a properly convened investigative authority and raising her hand, she swore to "facts" which later proved to be knowingly untrue. She got caught (metaphorically and actually) with her pants down.

When an officer is involved in a social relationship (sexual or not) with enlisted people, the Air Force (and all the other services) always considers a breech of discipline and a potential compromise of authority to be highly likely. Lt. Flinn was well educated in this philosophy during her four years at the Air Force Academy. In spite of this, **she chose to have sexual relations with an enlisted man** stationed at Minot. Then, during the same year, she chose to have an extended sexual relationship with a civilian who was married to an enlisted female stationed at Minot. When ordered to stop living with the married man, she chose to defy that order and continue.

Finally, questioned under oath, she lied about the fact that she had continued to see the man she was ordered to stay away from. If the gender roles were reversed, she (he) would have been court marshaled, punished and discharged (just as scores of men in all the services have) without so much as a blurb in the local Minot newspaper. Media pundits expressed pious outrage at the Army drill sergeant affair where senior enlisted men had taken advantage of their authority and had relations with junior recruits.

The Air Force considers Lt. Flinn (similarly) to be an officer who potentially and perhaps actually misused her authority. **An acknowledged liar** and person of low moral turpitude, she disobeyed orders and misled a properly authorized investigative officer. She lied under oath--a military felony---and incidentally, **she admittedly engaged in prohibited fraternization which wreaks havoc to good order and discipline in a military unit**.

Now, as the Black army drill sergeant recently convicted for his misdeeds cried "discrimination," so does Lt. Flinn. That powerful defense always evokes the sympathy of the media, but clearly in her case, it is particularly disingenuous. In the eyes of the Air Force, Lt. Flinn is as bad a character as were the Army drill sergeants. In keeping with the new Army policy for female recruits, perhaps the Air Force should have all male enlisted move about the base in pairs, to avoid the potential of **abuse from sexually predatory female officers.** There is at least one enlisted married female at Minot who would concur with that.

At commissioning, military officers are expected, and agree to observe a higher code of conduct than the general enlisted and civilian population. Certainly that does not always happen, but exemptions from those higher expectations, based on race or gender are not in the interest of anyone but a hypocrite.

The media's failure to acknowledge the parallels between the Army sex scandals and Lt. Flinn puts them squarely in that category. Flinn was the first female B-52 pilot in the USAF. Flinn was discharged from the U.S. Air Force in 1997 after being charged with making a false statement, adultery, and disobeying orders. Flinn's trouble with the Air Force received widespread media attention at the time and was discussed in a U.S. Senate hearing on May 22, 1997.

CHAPTER 10

This Too Will Pass

Former Coast Guard members and others with ties to the Coast Guard Academy were praising the Academy's handling of its first court-martial, saying the firm action will help the school's reputation rebound. Many in the region with ties to the Academy said the fact the school did not hide the allegations and followed through with a court-martial would help its reputation rebound. "The Academy has excellent processes in place to deal with this," said John Maxham, Vice President of Development for the Academy Alumni Association. "The most important thing is it was handled in the proper fashion." Maxham is a Coast Guard Academy Graduate in the Class of 1966. He is a classmate of Merle James Smith, Junior, the first African American to graduate from the Academy. Commander Merle Smith, USCG (Retired) was the Individual Military Counsel for Cadet Webster Smith.

Judith Buttery, 50, of Oakdale and a former member of the Coast Guard Band, said the rape allegation was something other colleges and universities have dealt with for years. "It happens so often in every other place," Buttery said. "It's just one of those things the Coast Guard will have to deal with. The Coast Guard Academy will weather this storm."
Chris Morello of Norwich, the CAPT Paul Foyt Chapter co-president of the Coast Guard Academy Parents Association, called the incident disappointing, but was glad the Academy handled it well. "It's disappointing for the best of the cadets that work as hard and are dedicated and disciplined to have a few put a black mark on the school,"

Morello said. "It's not good to judge anything based on one decision or challenge."

I was not one of those praising the Coast Guard Academy for its handling of its first court-martial. It was appalling to me that it should have been a General Court-martial. I agreed with the Article 32 Investigating Officer that the charges could have been resolved at an Article 15 Captain's Mast. Non-judicial punishment would have been more than sufficient.

I felt that a great miscarriage of justice had occurred. The life and career of a very promising cadet had been sacrificed. There were no processes in place to deal with allegations of sexual assault. They were making them up as they went along. This was an experiment. I do not think it will ever happen again.

Fortunately for the family of Webster Smith there were some white knights in the wings watching what I considered a miscarriage of justice and an abuse of process. I am referring primarily to the law firm that took his case on appeal. The case was taken as a pro bono case by the Wilmer Cutler Hale and Dorr law firm.

In December of 2007 as we were waiting for the decision on appeal from the Coast Guard Court of Criminal Appeals, it occurred to me that the best Christmas present the Coast Guard could give to the Lawyers from the Wilmer Cutler Hale and Dorr law firm representing cadet Webster Smith would be to rule against them.

It appeared that the best payment the Law Firm could get for representing Webster Smith would be another chance to make history. Taking this case pro bono, it was obvious that they would not receive any direct financial compensation for their services; but, they already had more money than they can spend.

Far more than money, a chance to make history by arguing the case before the Supreme Court would have been just compensation.
I believed that they had followed this case from day one. They had a premonition of its precedent setting nature. When would another case of this unique nature come along? Not in a thousand years. Like God up in

Heaven, hoping that Pharaoh would not give in and let the Hebrews go free, just so He could give the world repeated displays of his awesome power, Wilmer Cutler Hale and Dorr may have been secretly in its heart of hearts hoping the Coast Guard was as perverse as some had said that they were. That would give Wilmer Cutler Hale and Dorr a chance to make it to the Supreme Court to argue a really very simple and easy case of the wrongful prosecution of the first Black Cadet at the Coast Guard Academy.

Now, that would be a trophy worth more than a million dollar retainer. That would add a modern and impressive new paragraph to their website. They would continue to stroll down the corridors of history as the nation's preeminent civil rights law firm.

Knowing the Coast Guard as I did, I felt reasonably certain that they are about to get the number one item on their Christmas Wish List; that is, a chance to argue before the United States Supreme Court on behalf of a poor Black boy from Texas who had been abused by the military justice system. Little did I know at the time that the case would be appealed to the Supreme Court, only to have the nation's court of last resort deny the appeal with not one word of explanation. Could it be that the Court-martial of Webster Smith was just intended to attract media attention? Was Admiral James Van Sice trying to send a message to **U. S. Representative Christopher Shays** and the Pentagon and the other 3 military academies that this is how the Coast Guard Academy handles sexual assaults?

Former Congressman Shays, from Connecticut, a 10-term incumbent who lost a re-election bid in November 2008, was a conscientious objector during the Vietnam War. He never wore a military uniform. He is a good friend of **Richard Blumenthal**, a former Democratic senator from Connecticut, who had drawn scrutiny for saying he served in Vietnam when he actually received deferments between 1965 and 1970 and then joined the Marine Reserve.

At the very moment that the court-martial of Webster Smith was underway, U.S. Rep. Christopher Shays, a Connecticut Republican and chairman of the Subcommittee on National Security, Emerging Threats and International Relations, was holding a hearing concerning how officials were handling sexual assault cases in the military and its academies. The Hearings were held in Washington, D.C.. Coast Guard **Rear Admiral Paul J. Higgins from the Coast Guard Academy was on the witness list.**

Military officials said they have worked hard to improve critical areas such as victim support and confidentiality while providing training for all cadets to prevent sexual harassment and assault. Congress created a task force in 2004 that recommended many such changes. "The Air Force Academy has come a long way in addressing sexual assault and violence since the events of 2003 and before," Brig. Gen. Susan Y. Desjardins, Air Force Academy commandant of cadets, said in prepared testimony. But Shays suggested that more needed to be done: "We must provide an environment in the military at large that does not condone hostile attitudes and inappropriate actions toward women," Shays said. (Note 17)

It is strangely ironic that in April 2006 Representative Shays hosted a briefing on Capitol Hill where a former female Coast Guard Academy cadet, **Caitlin Stopper**, told of how her life became an "absolute hell" after she accused a fellow cadet of sexually assaulting her. Ms Stopper said that Academy officials tried to blame her for the alleged attack. (Note 16) Her attacker was white. He was allowed to quietly resign his cadet appointment. One has to wonder, if the rapist had been a Black cadet, would he have been allowed to quietly resign; or, would he have received a General Court-martial? That was truly a rape case. The Webster Smith case was not.

And then, along came Webster Smith. He was Black. The age of blaming the alleged victim, apparently was over. Since the Academy had excellent processes in place to deal with things like this, it was time to crank up the machinery. The most important thing was that it had to be handled in the proper fashion, but it was time to paint a face on crime at the Coast Guard Academy, that crime being sexual assault. This appeared to be an ideal case for racial profiling. <u>Racial profiling</u> is what happens when you take a set of circumstances associated with a certain crime and used them to identify the type of person likely to commit it.

CHAPTER 11

The True Profile of The Coast Guard Academy's Sexual Predator

Rapes have occurred at the Coast Guard Academy or onboard the Academy training ship, USCGC Eagle since as far back as 1977. From 1993 until the spring semester of 2005, the Coast Guard Academy had 10 reported incidents of sexual misconduct, according to information provided by the CGA. If we were to profile all of the sexual assailants from 1977 until the **Caitlin Stopper** sexual attack, we would get a composite of who should be the poster child for sexual assault at the Coast Guard Academy.

This is what we would get. He would be a white male between the ages of 17 and 21. He would be intelligent and athletic, but he would tend to be an introvert except when he has consumed a small amount of alcohol. Being something of a social misfit, he would prey on lonely or homely girls who solicited his assistance. Typically he would be asked for assistance with homework or with some aspect of an athletic skill that he had excelled at. These situations would tend to lure the unsuspecting female into his orbit of greatest achievement. His superior abilities in these areas would tend to bolster his confidence and give him the courage to mount an assault. Afterwards he would be able to convince himself that she asked for it, or he could fantasize that she came on to him. It was all her fault. He would feel little or no guilt.

This is a true story. The names have been changed to protect the privacy of the innocent. It has absolutely nothing to do with Webster Smith; except, of course, it demonstrates most vividly that the military justice apparatus at the Coast Guard Academy under Admiral James Van Sice and Captain Doug Wisniewski was running on two separate and very unequal tracks.

White rapists were dealt with underlined administratively and were allowed to resign from the Academy. The reporting females were harassed out of the Academy. An innocent Black cadet was framed, prosecuted, and sent to jail on perjured testimony. He was not given the administrative option. He was punished criminally. His accusers received plush assignments and other rewards.

The facts are as follows. One night a dainty little female distance runner was studying with her classmate in his room when without warning she was pounced on and savagely raped by three beefy bullies. Only one actually did the dirty deed, but the other two vicarious varmints are equally culpable. They not only failed to assist this damsel in distress, but they refused to raise a hue and cry for help. And against every human instinct for compassion, when questioned later, they lied about the incident. They were so distracted in their little 12 foot by 12 foot room that they were totally unaware that this delicate little flower had been deflowered.

The big bad burly football player who actually did the dirty deed, let's call him Mister Big, or MB for short. He was so brazen as to actually threaten the delicate flower and her two roommates with physical violence if they breathed a word about what he had done. The poor little innocent roommates of the delicate flower were so stressed that they were driven to take prescription medication. They even had to be referred for mental health counseling to cope with the somatic manifestations of the stress brought on by MB's threat.

Our delicate flower received no charity from her fellow cadets, both male and female. She became a pariah. She was branded and taunted by some of the other athletes. She had to face daily taunts of "What's the matter; <u>don't you like rough sex</u>?" Can you imagine such treatment from the cream of the crop?

She was ridiculed and branded a slot, harlot, loose woman, and not only by the other cadets. She was dragged out of bed one night about midnight in only her pajamas, and she was hauled before a Chief Petty Officer and a Lieutenant and she was called a bunch of dirty names. One can only imagine if this is how we treat victims of sexual assault today. Captain Doug Wisniewski did not call this rape; nor did he call it sexual assault. He called it <u>non-consensual sexual activity</u>. That way, he did not have to convene a court-martial. The Academy replaced Doug Wisniewski with a female Commandant of Cadets, Captain Judy Keene. She wanted to get female officers involved in the rape investigation and counseling process as early as possible. Captain Wisniewski said that there was an atmosphere of fear and intimidation at the Academy, and that some female cadets were hesitant to come forward with assault allegations.

On this point, I was in total agreement with Captain Wisniewski. But, the big question was, who were they afraid of? From what happened to our delicate flower after her rape, it is clearly obvious that they were afraid of the Academy staff officers.

This was incredible. Little did the news media realize when Captain Wisniewski said that there was <u>an atmosphere of fear and intimidation at the Academy,</u> that the female cadets were afraid of the officers. They were not afraid of Webster Smith. They were afraid of Doug Wisniewski and his staff officers. They were so afraid that they were willing to be used to court-martial Webster Smith, A real rapist and sexual predator, Mr. Big, had been allowed to slip away with nary a slap on the wrist.

This is the sad part of this story. What did they do to our delicate flower? First, Captain Wisniewski assigned a female staff officer to <u>interview</u> her. The interview turned into an <u>interrogation</u>. The interrogation became an <u>inquisition</u>. The female staff officer inferred that the delicate flower <u>was responsible for her own rape</u>. She, as much

98

as, accused her of provoking the incident. When the interview became a custodial interrogation, the delicate flower was not provided with legal counsel; nor was she given any Article 31 warnings. She was <u>forced to make a statement</u>, which <u>she did not write.</u> She <u>signed a statement</u> that the female staff officer had written and she <u>was not provided with a copy</u> of the statement. That statement went straight to Captain Wisniewski, and he used it in an Article 15 Non-Judicial Punishment Proceeding to expel a first class cadet two weeks before he was to graduate in the Class of 2006.

Who was this first class cadet? He was not Mr. Big, the person who had raped her. He was a senior cadet assigned to counsel the victim. He was showing some trained initiative and leadership, but apparently he fell in love with her. He was <u>charged with fraternization</u> and expelled two weeks before graduation. The System was on its head. It had turned upside down. It appeared that the inmates were in charge of the asylum. What happened to our delicate flower <u>on the night of the rape</u>? She was treated at a medical facility. She was taken off base, of course. We must always leave room for plausible deniability. Yes, she received expert civilian medical care.

The <u>physical evidence of the rape</u> was sent to the Connecticut Crime Laboratory. The lab report went to the New London Police Department. Captain Wisniewski sent a couple of his boys over when the Chief of Police was not in, and they <u>confiscated the forensic evidence</u> and took it back to the Academy. Perhaps, they screamed federal supremacy or something and walked out with the evidence.

What did Doug Wisniewski do with the forensic evidence? Heaven only knows. It certainly was not used to make an air-tight case against Mr. Big. This would have been a slam-dunk case to prosecute at a court-martial. But, no, Captain Wisniewski had Cadet Webster Smith in isolation waiting for a court-martial with only rumors and lies as evidence. So, in December 2005 CAPT Wisniewski takes MB to a Captain's Mast NJP and lets him resign from the Academy. He probably thought he was home free.

Now, our delicate flower was left in the hot house. All of the other female cadets saw what the Administration was doing to her. The Administration tried to get her to resign. The other female cadets became afraid and intimidated. Female cadets from freshmen to senior cadets were scared to death. They were more than happy to cooperate with Captain Wisniewski and facilitate the court-martial of Cadet Webster Smith.

Morale was at an all time low. Esprit de Corps had gone out the window. All the cadets became suspicious of each other. And they are all afraid of the Administration. The women were afraid to report incidents of any nature for fear of being forced to resign. The men were afraid that innocent incidental contact with a female cadet would lead to charges, false statements, and possible court-martial. That was the atmosphere of fear and intimidation that Captain Wisniewski had mentioned. He had created it himself.

According to a 2008 General Accounting Office Report, from 2003 to 2006 there were NO sexual-harassment complaints at the Coast Guard Academy, but there were 12 incidents of sexual assault reported to the Coast Guard Investigative Service (CGIS), with one incident in 2003, one in 2004, "NONE" in 2005 and 10 in 2006. The 10 incidents reported in 2006 would appear to have occurred after the Webster Smith court-martial. Webster Smith was removed from Chase Hall in 2005. Who was doing all of the sexual assaulting in 2006? Why were none of these people brought to justice? They could have been tried along with Webster Smith.

CHAPTER 12

An Eye Witness Account from A Female Inside Chase Hall

This is an unsolicited account from a former female Coast Guard Academy cadet. It adds a chilling perspective.

QUOTE:

Hi,

Please excuse my rambling. I think it's fascinating what you're doing. I hope more former cadets post. Who knows what insane things you witnessed and experienced at Chase Hell.

A little about myself...I am a black female ex-cadet who chose to walk away from Chase Hall in the mid-late 90's. I'm not that much older than Smith as I have younger sisters his age. I am now the mother of an extremely handsome toddler. With a son, this case hits home even more. The only other person I've discussed this case with was another friend of mine, who chose to stay on and graduate. Needless to say, even though I didn't graduate, I have an interesting perspective (non-legal, more social).

I read everything I possibly could about this case and only today found your blog. Here comes my laundry list of points....boy did Ms. Ringle hate those....

Point of view as a former cadet.

No, from reading the information in the papers, the case seemed thin. Why try this case and waste time and money? Could it be to save careers and get promotions at the expense of others? It happens. It seemed that there had been national pressure to start treating rape investigations as criminal investigations and not some Leave it to Beaver Wardroom prank. Someone had to be made an example of. Smith was easily casted as the villain. Lascivious, sociopathic, cad? (at least from my pov)....You bet. Rapist? I don't know....in the narrow elitist minds, his actions and "dating" patterns fit the bill of the some (not ALL) cadre's stereotypical fears of the "typical black thug criminal who are chasing after white women."

Could reg row princess have been humiliated for carrying a black baby? What if mummy and daddy found out? Better cry rape and justify the abortion. Just because you're a cadet, doesn't make you a human by any definition. Yes, possibly, not 100% sure.

I was glad, up until now rape allegations seemed to be taking on the nature of crim. investigations, rather than blaming the woman and sending everyone packing. This was a crappy case to choose.

You are also right in your posts about countless other rape cases, with physical evidence never going to trial with the alleged perps being allowed to quietly resign. I can think of at least 2 as if it were yesterday when I attended. I can also think of Cases where women screamed rape to save their hides when caught in the act. (In fact, my reluctant involvement in such a case was one of the final reasons why I decided to call it a day.)

From my experience, stuff rolled downhill. The rules were applied at whim to suit the purposes of whomever was in charge at the time. Discrimination against minorities was almost never overt. Exception, verbal stereotypes. A black male cadet could get a class 1 and a honor board hearing for a water gun prank in the mid 90's. I find it hard to believe that things had changed all that much. What was he thinking? Never mind.

I certainly didn't have all the time on my hands to party like it's 1999? What the h#$% going on at CGA? I'm curious to know, even though he was a firstie granted, where was the self-policing from the other black cadets. Behavior like this would have been cause for alarm. Since there were so few of us, we looked out for each other, even if we didn't really like our fellows. This nice little informal system was there years ago. Just curious about this.

As a parent of a little boy...

I have little doubt that Smith's parents "raised him right." I'm sure they warned him of potential situations like this. Sometimes, children make many outrageous mistakes. I wish that people in the black community and in the media would lay off. Separating oneself or relatives from the academy, let alone under these circumstances, is a mind job. The family will need time to grieve and deprogram. (blackamericaweb.com interview disregarded. I'd be p.oed too under the circumstances. I doubt I would have handled the trial with as much graciousness and class. True charges or not, the street language would have re-appeared, especially towards the commandant and accusers.) I raise my son to love your neighbor as yourself and to fall in love with whomever God sends to you, regardless of "race." Although I hope he would display more character, morals, and common sense than Smith and his accusers, I would be afraid to send him off to CGA at age 18 under these circumstances. It seems like the targeting has now worsened as a result of the trial. Things may get worse before they get better. Like it or not, just treatment at the hands of the officer corps or not, Smith brought this on himself and now made other black cadets lives more difficult. Yes, forgive me, I am angry at him for not knowing what they're capable of and most importantly, for being an out of control hormonal twit. Forget about when acting as wild as he was. Don't go where you eat!

All this having been said, I've witnessed the UCMJ process as I live in a military community as a spouse. UCMJ is even less just than the civilian system. It seems like the Smith verdict said "We can't prove you're guilty of rape, so we're going to convict you of something for getting this far." Especially with these NASTY charges, this probably wouldn't have gone to trial in the civilian world. If he was railroaded, TOTALLY POSSIBLE, I hope those in the legal community keep the pressure on those responsible for this legal mess. Who knows which cadet could be next for something even less severe.

Oh yes, I think one of the cadets leaked this investigation to the press, not necessarily the Commandant.

That's it. You'll all can rip my opinions. Won't be worse than the public evisceration Smith received.

Thanks, this blog is cool. Please forgive my spelling, format, slang and grammar.

D.M.Boyd

UNQUOTE

CHAPTER 13

We Are Doing The Right Thing

Academy's first female Commandant of Cadets is confident of her ability to set the proper course .
By Richard Rainey

Published on 8/6/2006
Capt. Judith Keene (CGA Class 1981) has deep roots in the Coast Guard here, having graduated from the academy and later commanded Coast Guard Station New London.

'Everything about the culture defied the presence of women at that time, really everything. And so it could become very isolating.'
Director of Admissions Capt. Susan Bibeau

Members of the United States Coast Guard Academy class of 2008 are formally accepted into the Corps of Cadets during a ceremony Wed. Aug. 18, 2004 on the academy's Washington Parade Grounds.

THE chance to flout a gender barrier did not call a young Judith Keene to attend the U.S. Coast Guard Academy 29 years ago. Nor did it spur on her long and varied career in uniform.

Nonetheless, she did break a barrier this summer when she became the first woman to serve as the academy's commandant of cadets.

Now a captain, Keene is moving into her campus office during a pivotal time in the academy's 130-year history. On the eve of the 30th anniversary of women cadets first lining up for drills and attending classes with men, the academy is taking stock after the turmoil left by the first general court-martial of a cadet. Webster M. Smith, 23, of Houston, was convicted in June of extorting a female classmate for sexual favors.

Smith's trial left an aftershock rippling through the cadet corps, according to cadets and academy officials. Testimony and interviews with those involved revealed an underlying sense that female cadets felt either fearful about reporting incidents of sexual assault or hopeless that anything would be done if they did.

Assuaging those fears and enacting positive changes are two missions at the top of Keene's list.

"Bad things have happened here, but we are addressing them," she said. "We are going to deal with them, and we are doing the right thing."

Keene, who graduated in 1981, credited the women of the class before her with paving the way for a generation of female officers in the Coast Guard.

"We really owe them a lot," she said.

The Class of 1980 included the first 14 women to graduate from the academy. The changes they brought to the cadet culture, changes Keene said she took for granted as a student only a year later, were significant for their ordinariness: a beautician in the campus barbershop who knew how to cut women's hair; uniform trousers made for women; nascent athletic teams, stretching from a champion women's sailing team to an ill-advised gymnastics team (only one woman in the original class had any background in the sport).

By graduation, that first class had lost 24 of the 38 women who donned uniforms in the summer of 1976. The women who stayed endured persecution in both harsh and subtle forms, said Capt. Susan Bibeau, a member of that class who is now the academy's director of admissions.

"Everything about the culture defied the presence of women at that time, really everything," she said. "And so it could become very isolating."

Interviews with former cadets and news reports from that time described misogyny among the cadets sometimes manifested in obscene language and ostracism. Women said they did not band together for fear of being accused of collusion.

"We did realize – in my case, two weeks into it – we were up against a different challenge, one we hadn't thought of," Bibeau continued. "We realized that we were actually pioneering. ... and I think most had to decide, are we going to take on that baggage or not?"

The women who did stick it out at the academy led the way for others to come.

"Over the years, there was almost like a shift even then. There were women in every class, and everything seemed normal," said Jean Wilczynski of Old Lyme, who graduated from the academy in 1983. "And even though there were still people who felt women shouldn't be there, it was very clear we were there."

Now women equal men at the academy in achievement and in the chain

107

of command, and some women have ascended to elite positions in the cadet corps. Last semester's regimental commander – the highest militarily ranked cadet – was a woman.

"Here at the Coast Guard Academy we do a really good job at keeping everything level," said Cadet DeCarol Davis, president of the junior class, in a recent interview.

Raw data from a survey by academy officials in August 2005 revealed that nearly half the senior female cadets did not know they could report a sexual assault confidentially to a counselor.

Ten women at the academy reported 18 incidents of sexual assault in the survey, entitled the "Human Relations Climate Survey of Cadets." Of those women, five thought the formal procedures offered by the academy helped them deal with the incidents.

Smith or his accusers might have been involved in some of the complaints, said an academy spokesman. A team of Pentagon analysts from the Defense Equal Opportunity Management Institute, which plans to look at the data later this month, should be able to make that determination.

In Smith's trial, five current or former female cadets testified that the senior cadet and former football player had inappropriately touched them. One woman, his former girlfriend, accused him of rape. Four of the women testified they had been drinking with Smith during the alleged incidents.

After eight days in the makeshift courtroom at the academy, Smith was convicted of extortion, sodomy and indecent assault in connection with only one of his accusers. The rape charge was dropped. He is now serving a six-month sentence in a Navy brig while awaiting an appeal.

On June 28, during Smith's sentencing, Capt. Douglas J. Wisniewski testified in writing that Smith's actions sent "fear and suspicion" through the corps of cadets. Wisniewski, now stationed at Coast Guard headquarters in Washington, D.C., was Keene's predecessor.

"Female cadets expressed their opinions that reporting sexual misconduct is not worth the personal toll on their lives," Wisniewski wrote.

Alcohol consumption and carousing among 18- to 22-year-olds is nothing beyond the scope of life on most college campuses, said Bibeau, who returned to the school to head the admissions department in August 2001.

But the academy is a military institution funded by the U.S. Department of Homeland Security, which is ultimately funded by taxpayer dollars. The school holds itself to a higher standard, she said.

The percentage of female cadets in the student body has hovered between 28 percent and 32 percent since 1999. It is the highest percentage of its kind among the nation's four military academies.

However, the incoming freshman class – the Class of 2010 – is 23 percent female. While reasons for the decline are only speculation at this point, Bibeau surmised that it could be a combination of an effort by the other academies to attract more women and the blow to the school's reputation landed by Smith's court-martial. She pointed out that she had received very few inquiries about the trial from prospective students.

Sitting at the long table in her office during a mid-July interview, Keene, 46, said she felt "energized" by her new wards, the 980-odd cadets who will march through the academy's gates in mid-August.

Keene's curriculum vitae appears tailor-made to help guide the prestigious academy as it assesses its policies. Tucked among her plans is what she hopes will clear the apparent confusion among women students about reporting sexual harassment or assault.

"We're going to be placing strict emphasis on our core values: honor, respect and devotion to duty," she said.

Keene entered the academy in 1977. A tall, blonde 17-year-old from Florida who grew up in a strict household, she fell in love with the lifesaving mission of the Coast Guard. She was also in love with her boyfriend at the time, she said, who spurred her application to the school through his own desire to attend.

"That was our plan, we were going to go together," she said.

She got in. He, however, did not. But by that point, Keene said, she knew what to expect from the smallest of the nation's four military academies.

"I knew it was going to be hard," she said. "You can't look through the Coast Guard Academy yearbook without getting a sense of some of the challenges you're going to have to face."

After graduation, she served on various ships and in a diverse array of commands. She earned her master's degree in business administration from the University of Hawaii. She is familiar with New London, having commanded the Coast Guard Station here from 1991 to 1994. And she knows the challenges women face in uniform; she served as the gender policy adviser to the commandant of the Coast Guard for two years.

The new commandant of cadets ascribes to what she called "the broken window theory." It is a philosophy that for more than two decades has governed many city police departments. It postulates that a deteriorated environment leads to disorder among its inhabitants.

With that in mind, Keene said, she will place renewed emphasis on the "basics" among the cadets – from proper attire to clean bunks and decorum at the dinner table.

"If you enforce just the basic bottom line rules and regulations, and you do it constantly and consistently, it's a lot easier to enforce the larger things," she said.

To handle those larger things, especially reports of sexual assault and harassment at the school, Keene said she has planned roundtable discussions and focus groups for cadets.

Keene also said she will return direct command of the cadets to commissioned lieutenants to ramp up supervision. For the past four years, the academy implemented a leadership strategy in which upperclassmen were the first line of discipline for students.

Beyond the changes, Keene said she sensed optimism among the returning cadets.

"They are enthusiastic, and they are very proud of what they have individually and collectively accomplished," she said. "And I think they are looking ahead as well."

CHAPTER 14

No Review, No Comment By The Supreme Court

The U.S. Supreme Court refused to hear the appeal of Webster Smith. The justices declined to hear the case without comment. The decision of the Court of Appeals for the Armed Forces (CAAF) has become the final decision in the case.

That is a shame because the military justice court-martial and the appeal system is not race neutral. A seemingly race neutral system has operated to deny minority members of the armed forces the equal protection of law. Institutional racism and racial profiling operating in a culture that evolved under the system of slavery have reduced Black appellants to a stereotype and disproportionately predetermines that they will be convicted and that they will not prevail on appeal.

The Writ of Certiorari is the writ that an appellate court issues to a lower court in order to review its judgment for legal error and review, where no appeal is available as a matter of right. Since the Judiciary Act of 1925, most cases cannot be appealed to the U.S. Supreme Court as a matter of right; therefore, a party who wants that court to review a decision of a federal or state court files a "petition for writ of certiorari" in the Supreme Court. If the court grants the petition, the case is scheduled for the filing of briefs and for oral argument.

Since the Coast Guard is in the Department Of Homeland Security, Smith had the right to submit additional information to Secretary of Homeland Security Janet Napolitano before she approved his sentence. Smith also had the right to seek a new trial before the Coast Guard Court of Criminal Appeals. He would have had to submit new evidence that had not already been considered in the case. He could also have had his record cleaned with a presidential pardon. Since he was a resident of Texas he had to register as a sex offender. One Judge on the Coast Guard Court of Criminal Appeals found that former cadet Webster Smith was denied a fair trial and that the case should have been sent back to the trial court for a new trial. He found that the Case of United States vs Webster Smith should have been returned to the Convening Authority for a new trial. The Judge found so many discretionary errors in the court-martial proceedings that he had no choice but to rule that <u>Webster Smith had been denied a fair trial.</u> It was a classic case of <u>"he-said, she-said"</u>. The trial came down to simply a **credibility issue**. The **big question** was who was telling the truth and who was not. **This was a question for the jury to decide**. It was **a fact question**. The jury is the trier of facts. The court-martial judge (CAPT Brian Judge) went to extraordinary lengths to keep the question out of the hands of the jury. He took it upon himself to decide the issue of credibility. **That was a major contributing factor as to why Webster Smith was convicted.**

The jury had no idea what the real issue was. They were kept in the dark. They were not given proper instructions. The judge decided who was the more credible witness. The judge abused his discretion. The judge went beyond the authority and power delegated to him under the Uniform Code of Military Justice (UCMJ), and the Federal Rules of Evidence. Webster Smith was denied his Sixth Amendment Rights.

One does not have to read the Appeals Court decision to know that an accused at a court-martial has a right to cross-examine the witnesses against him. Anyone who has watched Perry Mason or Tom Cruise in the movie "A Few Good Men", would come away with an appreciation for the fact that the jury has the responsibility to decide what the facts are and who is not telling the truth.

When a judge does not allow the jury to do its job, he commits **reversible error**. When a judge confuses his duties with the duties assigned to the jury, then he has abused his discretion and that constitutes reversible error.

The **prosecution was allowed** to ask Webster Smith questions that were like bombshells that would cave in the sides of a Sherman Tank, but on cross-examination of the principal witness, the Defense lawyers were reduced to tip-toeing through the tulips. The uncorroborated testimony of the principal witness (SR) was a roadside bomb to Webster Smith's defense.

If the jury had only been allowed to follow the Yellow Brick Road and to resolve the credibility issue itself, then, at least, the trial of Webster Smith would have had some semblance of a fair trial. The trial judge, CAPT Brian Judge, was not taking any chances. He took matters into his own hands. He jumped onto the Scales of Justice and pulled them way down on the side of the Prosecution.

In a case where the principal witness was allowed to hide behind the military judge for protection from thorough cross-examination; and where facts and perceptions may have been dispositive of the ultimate issue, **Truth** can be elusive. In a case where a convincing and charming fabricator of facts can sway a jury that has not been fully informed, and where the jury has only been given some of the relevant facts, the judge left a lot of room for mischief on the part of a sneaky prosecutor. The judge left a lot of room for the imagination of the jury to run wild when he allowed the Prosecutor to introduce just enough evidence to put Webster Smith in a compromising position; but he denied the Defense lawyers an opportunity to explain the contradictions by cross-examining the principal witness. Then the judge left it to the jury to "connect the dots". This was terribly unfair to the accused, Webster Smith.

114

Webster Smith was reduced to "a bug under a glass jar" for inspection, and the principal witness was kept as snug as a bug in a rug. Eventually all of this discretionary "hokus-pokus" became so egregious as to eliminate any possibility of a fair trial for Webster Smith. Finding the Truth became next to impossible. This case should have been remanded for a new trial. To send the case back to the Superintendent of the Coast Guard Academy, the Convening Authority, for a new trial was the only fair way to remedy the errors that were committed in the court-martial of Webster Smith.

The Founding Fathers and the framers of the U S Constitution provided procedural safeguards for criminal defendants facing the awesome powers on the Federal Government. They gave him; among other rights, the right to remain silent, the right to trial by jury, and the right to confront and to cross-examine the witnesses against him. These rights are inalienable. These rights cannot be taken away; not by the Government, and certainly not by a part-time trial judge.

One judge on the Coast Guard Court of Criminal Appeals saw clearly how the legal system, the Sixth Amendment to the Constitution, and the Military Rules of Evidence were misused to deny Webster Smith a fair trial.

I believe a great travesty of justice was committed. A gross miscarriage of justice was done at the Coast Guard Academy. The entire process was flawed. The only evidence was the word of a couple of incredible females. There was no physical evidence whatsoever. Webster Smith has apologized for his behavior. Confession is good for the soul. It is the first step toward true rehabilitation. No one else involved in the entire episode showed such strength of character. The Academy is a character building institution.

Cadet Webster Smith was a victim of jealousy, racial discrimination, a violation of the 14th Amendment Equal Protection clause, and last but not the least, a victim of a double standard. He was one of the most loved and respected cadets on campus. But he had two things going against him. One, he had dated the first female Regimental

Commander, and the Dean of Admissions' daughter. Both were white. Since they were white and Cadet Smith was Black, it did not sit well with the Commandant of Cadets. Racial Prejudice is still very much alive at the Academy.

America's fighting men have come in many guises, shapes and sizes. They have had to fight all of America's enemies, both foreign and domestic. Cadet Webster Smith had to fight his own senior officers, friends, and mentors. In the end he was proud. He had fought the good fight. Even TIME magazine carried the quote of the first cadet in Coast Guard history to be tried by a General Court-martial. (http://www.time.com/time/quotes/0,26174,1209244,00.html) Less than 60 days after the verdict was rendered in the Webster Smith case, I predicted that the case would make it all the way to the Supreme Court.

Supreme Court justices are not elected. They are appointed with the advice and consent of the Congress. The Nine Justices of the Supreme Court are the least democratic branch of the federal government. They have no constituency. They do not have to conform to the biases of the majority. They are the Court of Last Resort; so, they are infallible. With few exceptions, they have dealt with evenhandedly with all of America's citizens.

They do not have to sit for re-election. They are appointed for life. They are totally isolated from busy bodies on the Right or Left Side of the political spectrum. With one stroke of the pen, they may act to curb injustices, correct unsavory attitudes, and breathe new life into a living Constitution.

Historically we have looked to them to solve our most vexing social problems. They are America's ultimate arbiters of justice; and, that includes military justice. Aside from the Webster Smith Case, I cannot think of any case or incident in Coast Guard history that affected more directly the hearts, minds, and daily lives of all members of the United States Coast Guard.

The U.S. Coast Guard Court of Criminal Appeals had to review the Webster Smith case. It had no choice. Article 66 of the Uniform Code of Military Justice, requires the Coast Guard Criminal appeals Court to review all cases of trial by court-martial in which the sentence as approved by the Convening Authority extends to dismissal of a cadet from the Coast Guard, and/or a dishonorable or bad conduct discharge, unless the accused waives appellate review. Webster Smith did not waive appellate review. He appealed his conviction. Oral arguments in the Case of The Appeal of the Court-martial Conviction of Cadet Webster Smith was scheduled for January 16, 2008 in Arlington, Virginia.

A legal brief filed by his lawyers claimed the convictions should have been thrown out because the defense team was not allowed to fully cross-examine one of his accusers during Smith's court martial. They said that meant the jury didn't hear testimony that the accuser, a female cadet, Shelly Roddenbush, had once had consensual sex with a Coast Guard enlisted man and then called it sexual assault. If she lied once, she very well could have lied again.

The Coast Guard Court of Criminal Appeals is made up of Coast Guard Officers. It has the power to decide matter of both fact and law. Decisions of the Coast Guard Court of Criminal Appeals may be appealed to the Court of Appeals of the Armed Forces (CAAF). It is made up of five civilian judges, appointed to 15 year terms. It decides only issues of law. Its decisions may be appealed to the U. S. Supreme Court. The Webster Smith Case followed this long and winding path all the way to the Supreme Court.

The U.S. Supreme Court refused to hear the appeal of Webster Smith. The justices declined to hear the case without comment. Webster Smith was proud of his decision to fight the good fight all the way to the end of the road. See TIME magazine June 29, 2006. http://www.time.com/time/quotes/0,26174,1209244,00.html Most Supreme Court watchers had expected the Supreme Court to hear the case or at the very least to give an explanation of why not. This case implicated a deep federal circuit conflict regarding the standard of review that applies when a trial judge's restriction on the cross-examination of a prosecution witness is challenged on appeal as a violation of the Confrontation Clause. The Court of Appeals for the Armed Forces (CAAF) held that the standard of review is abuse of discretion rather than de novo. Applying the former standard, the court rejected Webster Smith's Confrontation Clause claim by a vote of 3-2.

The Courts Of Appeals Are Deeply Divided Over What Standard Of Review Applies To Confrontation Clause Claims Like Webster Smith's. The CAAF employed abuse-of-discretion review in resolving Smith's Sixth Amendment challenge to the military judge's restriction on the defense's cross-examination of SR. That approach conflicts with the holdings of five circuits, which consider comparable Confrontation Clause claims de novo, reserving abuse-of-discretion review for non-constitutional challenges. For example, the Seventh Circuit has stated that "[o]rdinarily, a district court's evidentiary rulings are reviewed for abuse of discretion.

> However, when the restriction [on cross-examination] implicates the criminal defendant's Sixth Amendment right to confront witnesses against him, ... the standard of review becomes de novo." The First, Fifth, Eighth, and Tenth Circuits have adopted the same approach. Six other circuits, by contrast—the Second, Third, Fourth, Sixth, Eleventh, and District of Columbia Circuits— Take the same approach that CAAF does, applying abuse-of-discretion review even when a restriction on the cross-examination of a prosecution witness is attacked on constitutional grounds. The Sixth Circuit, for example, stated in one case that "[defendant] argues that his right to confrontation was violated when the trial court 'unfairly' limited his cross-examination of [a] government witness .... We review the district court's restriction on a defendant's right to cross-examine witnesses for abuse of discretion."

In short, CAAF's use of an abuse-of-discretion standard in this case perpetuated a clear—and recognized—conflict in the circuits. **The**

Question Presented Was Recurring And Important, And The Smith Case Was A Good Vehicle For Deciding It.

The circuit conflict at issue warranted resolution by the Supreme Court. The constitutionality of restrictions on cross-examination arises frequently in criminal prosecutions, and in every part of the country. Those cases also show that the conflict over the standard for appellate review of such restrictions is established; there is no benefit to be gained by giving the lower courts additional time to consider the issue. Moreover, the question presented was important, because the standard of review can determine the outcome of an appeal. The difference between a rule of deference and the duty to exercise independent review is much more than a mere matter of degree. In even moderately close cases, the standard of review may be dispositive of an appellate court's decision. That is particularly true when one standard is highly deferential: CAAF, for example, has stated that "the abuse of discretion standard is a strict one," satisfied only when "[t]he challenged action [is] arbitrary, fanciful, clearly unreasonable, or clearly erroneous".

Also, non-uniformity created by the conflict directly affects a fundamental individual right. Some defendants in criminal cases enjoy less protection of the critical right to confront their accusers because of the fortuity of where their trials were held, or, as to cases decided by CAAF, because they have chosen to wear the nation's uniform.

The Webster Smith case presented a good vehicle to resolve the circuit conflict. Webster Smith's standard-of-review argument was both pressed and passed upon in the court of appeals, rendering the issue suitable for review by certiorari. In addition, CAAF's rejection of Smith's argument may well have determined the ultimate outcome. Even applying highly deferential review, CAAF was narrowly divided as to the constitutionality of the military judge's ruling in this case. If even one of the three judges who deemed that ruling not to be an abuse of discretion were to conclude, upon reviewing without deference, that it was inconsistent with the Sixth Amendment, Webster Smith would have prevailed.

Justice truly was not served in this case. American justice has been given a black eye. All American citizens cannot expect the equal protections of the law guaranteed by the United States Constitution. Even those who put on the uniforms of the Armed Forces of the United States of America and swear to defend and to protect the Constitution cannot rely upon its legal guarantees. The Case of Webster Smith is but one grain of sand upon the beaches of American justice. May God save us all from an experience like this at the bar of American justice.

CHAPTER 15

THE AFTERMATH

Webster Smith's faith in American Justice has been shattered. He is simply devastated. The patience of his family has been tested to the limit. His mother and father are coping with serious health related challenges brought on by the stress of this ordeal. This has been the most serious family crisis that Cleon and Belinda Smith have had to endure. The demands of daily work, uncertainty concerning the future of their son and his little infant daughter due to the consequences of having to register as a sex offender in Texas, the family has been put under enormous pressure. The family's support network and the friends of Webster Smith have all been stretched to the limit. This has affected their physical and mental health. A simple diet, rest, and exercise have had only minor success in relieving their symptoms.

The simple life style that Belinda and Cleon knew growing up was not available to Webster Smith and his wife and child. Something as simple as a birthday party for their daughter was not available to them. Webster could not attend a party for his daughter and a few of her close friends because of the restrictions imposed by the Texas sex offender law.

Captain Doug Wisniewski, the Commandant of Cadets, graduated from the Academy with the last all-male class. He was transferred to a position at Coast Guard Headquarters in Washington, D.C. and was replaced by the first woman to hold the post, Captain Judith Keene, who graduated in the second class to accept women.

Captain Judith Keene, the first female Commandant of Cadets pledged a tough stance against campus sexual violence in July 2006 following the court-martial in which cadets testified that such issues were not taken seriously.

Such attacks are "just reprehensible and I do not want to graduate a cadet into the Coast Guard as a junior officer who is a perpetrator of sexual assault," said Captain Keene.

The Coast Guard Academy had the first woman superintendent of a military service academy at the helm of the U.S. C. G. A. when classes convened in the summer of 2011. The commandant of the Coast Guard, Admiral Robert Papp, selected **Rear Adm. Sandra L. Stosz**, Coast Guard Director of Reserve and Leadership, for the Superintendent position. Rear Admiral Stosz **graduated** from CGA in **1982** with a Bachelor of Science degree in Government. She was the first female graduate of Coast Guard Academy to achieve flag rank. Stosz never married. She stated that her Coast Guard career was her lifetime adventure.

No good deed goes unpunished, it had been said. Webster Smith was a keeper of secrets, other peoples' secrets. In the end all the secrets came to light. When they did, there was betrayal of trust and tragedy for all parties to the secrets. Webster Smith kept the secret of KN's pregnancy and abortion during their senior year at the Academy. When he divulged her secret, KN set in motion events that led to his court-martial. He kept the secret of SR's illicit consensual sex with an enlisted man in Virginia during summer training. That secret led to his conviction.

A study by the Government Accountability Office (GAO) 2008 after a series of revelations about sexual misconduct at U.S. military academies, found that the Coast Guard is not required to report to Congress any measures taken to stem the tide of sexual assault and harassment cases the Coast Guard Academy. The GAO noted the Coast Guard Academy is the only U.S. military academy not required to report to Congress on sexual-misconduct cases.

According to the GAO Report, from 2003 to 2006 there were NO sexual-harassment complaints at the Coast Guard Academy, but there were 12 incidents of sexual assault reported to the Coast Guard Investigative Service, with one incident in 2003, one in 2004, "NONE" in 2005 and 10 in 2006.

The 10 incidents reported in 2006 would appear to have occurred after the Webster Smith court-martial. Webster Smith was removed from Chase Hall in 2005. Who was doing all of the sexual assaulting in 2006? Why were none of these people brought to justice? They could have been tried along with Webster Smith. There is something wrong with this picture. The GAO report suggests that CGA's figures may not tell the full story.

This GAO Report could have been used at the Webster Smith trial. At the very least, it could have been impeachment evidence against Doug Wisniewski, the Commandant of Cadets. He testified concerning an atmosphere of fear among the female cadets because of a sexual predator in Chase Hall.

How could that be? If there were NO reported incidents of sexual assault in 2005, from whence cometh the atmosphere of fear? If there had been any incidents of sexual assault,, surely they would have been reported, because CAPT Wisniewski was in charge of reporting them.

This same GAO Report could have been used to cross-examine every female who testified against Webster Smith. If any incident had occurred, why did they not report it? Did they forget? Was their memory better at the time of the alleged incident, or later at the court-martial?

Webster Smith was court-martialed in 2006. When was he supposed to have committed these offenses? The Investigation into his conduct began in 2005. The GAO report suggests that CGA's figures may not tell the full story. That is putting it mildly and politely. Thirteen female cadets and 11 males at the U.S. Coast Guard Academy (CGA) reported anonymously in an **April 2008 survey** that they experienced **"unwanted sexual contact," ranging from touching to forced sexual acts, during the 2007-08 school year.**

More than three-quarters said that **alcohol or drugs were involved** and that the offender was a fellow cadet. None of the women sought professional help and only 7 percent discussed the incident with authorities. Not enough of the male respondents answered follow-up questions to provide data, according to the Defense Department survey.

"The fact that we have **cadets who are being predators on cadets** bothers me because I'm committed to giving cadets a safe living and working environment," said **Capt. John Fitzgerald**, the new Commandant of Cadets. "I'm not going to rest until the day I leave here, working to eradicate that."

The last survey of cadets, done by CGA in October 2006, found that there were 23 incidents of sexual assault involving 14 women and nine men. Cadet focus groups revealed acceptance, and even encouragement, of alcohol use. A few months before that survey was taken, senior cadet **Webster Smith** was court-martialed on charges of sexual assault, among other things.

The Defense Department conducts a congressionally mandated **"service academy gender relations survey"** every two years at the West Point, Annapolis and the U.S. Air Force Academy. CGA, which falls under the Department of Homeland Security, voluntarily participated last year instead of doing its own survey of cadets.

Participating is a way to make CGA more transparent and to give Coast Guard officials an unbiased look at the state of gender relations at the school, **Fitzgerald** said. Cadets are told about the survey at a meeting and can choose whether or not to complete it.

It is difficult to draw comparisons between past CGA surveys and the DOD version because the surveys use different terminology, like "sexual assault" versus "unwanted sexual contact," and ask about different timeframes, such as a cadet's entire time at the academy versus one school year.

At the DOD academies, 9 percent of women and 1 percent of men reported experiencing some form of unwanted sexual contact last year, while 52 percent of women and 11 percent of men said they were sexually harassed. **At CGA, 44 percent of women and 14 percent of men reported being sexually harassed. More than three-quarters said the offender was a fellow cadet.**

"We can't have sexual harassment here, because you can't be a leader and have people look at you in two different lights," **Fitzgerald** said. "We have to get to a point where if that happens, another cadet will turn around and say, 'Stop. You are a Coast Guard cadet who will be a Coast Guard officer and you're supposed to be the epitome of a leader and a professional and you can't behave in this manner.' " (Note 21)

Is John Fitzgerald casted from the same mold as Doug Wisniewski? Will he court-martial another cadet? U. S. Coast Guard COMMANDANT INSTRUCTION 1754.10C (The Sexual Assault Prevention and Response Program) has been promulgated. The purpose of the program is to establish policy and prescribe procedures for the Coast Guard Sexual Assault Prevention and Response Program (SAPRP). The ultimate purpose of this program is to build a culture of prevention, sensitive response and accountability in keeping with the Coast Guard's values of honor, respect, and devotion to duty.

It appears that the message that the court-martial of Webster Smith was supposed to send was not received "loud and clear" by the intended parties. Or perhaps the cadets just cannot help themselves.

They continue doing what normal, healthy, red-blooded Americans have been doing since the dawn of time.

Could it be that the fault is not with the cadets but with the Administration? If you continue to place these attractive physical specimens in close proximity with each other, and force them to come together as a team, can you really expect them to act any differently? One definition of insanity is doing the same thing over and over and expecting a different result.

Civilian colleges do not appear to have the same problems, at least, not to the same degree. At civilian colleges students can inhabit the same physical environment and never really interact. They can remain individuals without developing a group identity. They do not live together, even in a dormitory. No one forces them to take group responsibility for the acts of any individual. Things are different at a military academy. Strangers are forced to become intimately aware of each other and to work together for a common goal. They bond and they develop a group identity. When one catches a cold, they all sneeze. They begin to take responsibility for each other; they become like family. A little touchy-feely is inevitable.

The most logical solution is to separate the genders. Put them on different floors or in different buildings. It might even be necessary to put them at separate training facilities. That is the only way to eliminate any possibility of unwanted touching. However, eventually they will have to come together for training and for work. That is when the temptations and the infatuations will begin. One person's unwanted sexual contact (sexual assault) can be another person's sexual fantasy. You never know until after the fact.

When Alexander Hamilton organized the Revenue Cutter Service in 1790 it was established in the Department of the Treasury. Later it became known as the Coast Guard. In 1966 it was placed in the Department of Transportation. Today it is the nucleus of the Department of Homeland Security. Webster Smith's case was reviewed for clemency by the Secretary of the Department of Home Land Security, Janet Napolitano. No Clemency was granted.

Webster Smith would have made an excellent military officer. It is Webster Smith and people like him that I want on the wall as our last line of defense for our American way of life protecting us from the great unwashed horde that is coming. Secretary Napolitano who do you want on that wall? Surely not people like former Congressman Christopher Shays, who has never worn the uniform of any branch of the American armed forces. Deferments and conscientious objections will not protect us when the enemy is at the gate.

Not everyone agreed with me concerning Webster Smith's potential to be a good Coast Guard Officer.

In July , 2006 in "Unsavory times at Academy,"
BD made the following poignant observations:

"So the U.S. Coast Guard Academy is marking its 30th year of admitting women. The first-ever cadet to be court-martialed is off to jail for extorting sexual favors. And the commandant of cadets has pledged to make it easier to report sexual infractions.

As a citizen and, especially as a woman, I suppose I should be happy that female peers of one Webster M. Smith forced him to face responsibility for his shameful conduct. Yet after repeated testimony by his accusers that they were either too drunk or too timid to stand up to him, it seems a fragile victory.

Late last month Smith was convicted of sodomy, which includes oral sex in the military's definition, extortion and indecent assault. He was acquitted of rape, a charge made by an on-again, off-again girlfriend who testified that she couldn't recall the rape because she had guzzled three liters of wine, vomited and passed out.

After the incident, which left her pregnant and led to an abortion, she had sex, admittedly consensual, with Smith again.

The extortion charge stemmed from another cadet's claim that after she told Smith about an act that could have brought her dismissal from the academy, he requested motivation to keep her secret. This led her to pose naked with him, she said, which they had joked about doing before, and to exchange oral sex with him.

Startlingly, testimony that Smith deleted the nude photo because its existence made the woman nervous revealed at least a modicum of decency on his part.

There are so many sad things about this trial, but the saddest of all, to me, is that it seemed to send a message that women want the freedom to act as recklessly as men, yet at the same time be protected from our own unique consequences.

Don't get me wrong: We women have every right, or at least the same right, to get drunk, have casual sex or make complete fools of ourselves, and none of this entitles men to do with us as they please.

But here's the thing: Men are usually stronger physically, and don't get pregnant. So equal opportunity to control the situation or escape the consequences of alcoholic stupor remains something of an ideal.

The young women in this case were rightfully not on trial, including in the media. That's progress. But I know I wasn't the only woman wondering, day after day, what did they think might happen if they put themselves in such a vulnerable position, and why were they so ill-equipped to deal with it?

Virtually all of us have slipped up, and you have to give the women credit for coming forth when their own part in all this was so embarrassing.

Maybe I've seen too many pictures of sloshed college women allowing themselves to be slobbered over and pawed at during spring break, but I found myself concerned that maybe they weren't embarrassed.

Then I had to ask myself, as a member of the generation that brought you the sexual revolution: What hath we wrought?

"Capt. Judith Keene, the first woman named commandant of cadets, wants to ensure that cadets feel free to report sexual harassment, and confident they'll be taken seriously. But if that's all the academy does, it's shirking its duty.

Although you can argue that the trial of Webster M. Smith didn't prove he was a criminal, it did show him to be untrustworthy, arrogant, and certainly no gentleman. According to the rules, that makes him unfit to be an officer in the U.S. Coast Guard.

The unspoken question, which only the academy can answer, is this: What does it mean, if it means anything at all, for a future U.S. military officer to act like a <u>lady</u>?"

<u>BD's</u> question was answered a few days later by **TMDW**. She said the following:

RE: Less-than-honorable Coast Guard Women

The column <u>"Unsavory times at Academy,"</u> by BD, published July 7, is right on the money. I thought I must be the only person wondering about the conduct of those female cadets. Although taking advantage of a woman is never acceptable, women should be cautioned to use discretion when drinking. To put yourself in the position of passing out from drinking is shameful, more so as a cadet and role model. When you allow yourself to be vulnerable, someone will take advantage of you, sexually or otherwise. This is exactly the type of risky behavior so much time and money is spent telling girls and women of all ages to avoid.

After all the hard work that goes into being at the Academy in the first place, you would think these women would be strong and confident leaders not sorority girls looking for a good time.

Why does the exchange of oral sex not mean a sodomy charge for the female involved? I have heard nothing of charges against the women at all. At a minimum they should all be dismissed from the Academy. If **Webster M. Smith is unfit to be an officer in the U.S. Coast Guard, then the women in this mess should be held accountable to the same degree**.

Good luck to the U.S. military if this is the nonsense we can look forward to in future officers.

/s/

TMDW

The tide of public opinion seems to have changed a bit since 2006 when Webster Smith was convicted. It took a lot of courage and conviction for Ms. TMDW to write that letter in 2006. At that time, she was bucking the tide of public sentiment. After sober reflection, and after the Case of The Conviction of Webster Smith has run the complete gauntlet from court-martial to the United Supreme Court in 2010, I am left with one question concerning the women in this case:

Was their behavior CONDUCT UNBECOMING an Officer and a Lady?

CHAPTER 16

A Simple Case of Black and White

The System does not work for everyone. It did not work for Webster Smith. He made love to his girlfriend and was charged with rape. During that year he assisted her in recovering from the residual effects of an abortion and continued to date her. **John K. Miller forcibly sexually assaulted a total stranger**, resulting in his receiving a broken nose; yet he remained on course, steady as she goes.

On Nov. 12, 2006 Coast Guard Cadet John K. Miller was arrested at the Navy Lodge hotel in Groton on charges of third-degree sexual assault, first-degree unlawful restraint and second-degree breach of peace. That cadet, John K. Miller, a 19-year-old from Michigan, was at a party with other cadets in a hotel when, police said, he assaulted a female guest, who is not a cadet. Police said there was alcohol at the two-room party. Miller had prevented his victim from leaving one of the rented motel rooms, police said, and **forced her to have sexual contact that was not traditional intercourse, according to one officer.**

When he was arrested, John Miller was bleeding and had sustained a broken nose. Whoever broke his nose must have been a pretty tough cookie. A 6 foot 2 inch 200 pound football player is no pushover, even when he has been drinking. The victim was not a member of the Track or Volley Ball team. She was a civilian.

Cadet Miller was treated at Lawrence Memorial Hospital. He was released into the custody of the Commandant of Cadets at the Coast Guard Academy after posting $10,000 bail.

Miller - a member of the academy football team - was in Superior Court in New London on Monday, December 4th, wearing a jacket and tie. He was not in his Coast Guard cadet uniform. He spoke with a judge for a moment, just long enough to have another appearance set: a Jan. 8 pretrial hearing. Leaving the courthouse, he chose not to comment on his case.

Miller continued attending classes and living in Chase Hall, the Academy barracks. That is a switch from the situation with Webster Smith, who was immediately removed from any exposure to other cadets, prevented from going to class, and forced to work at hard labor on the boat docks.

Cadet John K. Miller is a white Caucasian; whereas, Cadet Webster Smith is a Black African-American. They were both football player at the Academy, but that is where their similarities end. **Webster Smith was singled out for special punishment** and character assassination. His cadet photo was released to the news media early in the investigation process to achieve maximum exposure. Cadet John K. Miller was shielded from public exposure. He was not removed from the cadet barracks at Chase Hall. He continued to attend classes. He was not subjected to pre-trial punishment. Webster Smith was **forced to work at hard labor on the boat docks**. The treatment of the two cadets has been as different as night and day.

The ink was hardly dry on Admiral James Van Sice's Approval of the Sentence in the Webster Smith case when John Miller was arrested for sexual assault. The **Assistant Superintendent, Captain D. R. May, said** that the Smith case had shown resolve and **commitment to our system of military justice, accountability** and most important, our true embodiment of the **Coast Guard's core values** of **Honor, Respect and Devotion to duty**. He asserted that the Academy Superintendent would **never waiver from his commitment** to these precious values and would ensure that they would always be present in all that is done at the Coast Guard Academy.

It was really fortunate for Captain May that the John Miller was arrested for sexual assault at such an opportune time. It provided Captain May and the Academy senior staff with a timely and appropriate opportunity to **demonstrate their commitment to core values and to equal protection of laws**. Time has shown how selective they have been in living up to their own standards.

The accusations against Webster Smith were internal, so the investigation was conducted by the Coast Guard and ended in a military General Court-martial. Smith was placed in jeopardy of imprisonment for 20 years to life. In John K. Miller's case, he was arrested by Groton, Connecticut City Police and faced a criminal trial in civilian court.

On October 10, 2007 The Day reported the results of John K. Miller's civilian trial. If cadets John K. Miller and Steve Schimmel stay out of trouble, **the criminal cases** against them **will be dismissed**. John K. Miller and Steve Schimmel were arrested in separate incidents last fall and dismissed from the Academy in January 2007.

Miller was accused of sexually assaulting a person at a party and preventing the victim from leaving the room at the Navy Lodge on November 12, 2006. Groton Town police charged him with third-degree sexual assault, first-degree unlawful restraint and second-degree breach of peace. Police said Miller was among a group of people who had rented rooms at the lodge and were partying.

Miller was placed on a two-year form of special probation called accelerated rehabilitation in New London Superior Court on April 23, 2007. He cannot contact the victim or go to the academy. **He must also undergo an alcohol evaluation** and any other evaluation, counseling or treatment deemed necessary by the Office of Adult Probation. Miller and his attorney, Paul F. Chinigo of Norwich, declined to comment.

According to court documents, Miller's application for accelerated rehabilitation was granted because **the court believed he**

probably will not offend in the future; he has not been adjudicated as a youthful offender within the past five years; and he has **no previous record**. (**Webster Smith** had no prior record. As a matter of fact **he was a choir boy**)

The victim was notified of the agreement and the case was continued to April 24, 2009, when it was most likely dismissed and **Miller's <u>record absolved. This would allow Miller the option to apply for re-instatement as a cadet.</u>** (**Webster Smith was not afforded such an option, and he has been forced to carry the stigma of a registered sex offender.**)

Schimmel was accused of forcing his way on Oct. 29 into the house of a couple who said he was intoxicated at the time. New London police charged him with second-degree criminal trespass, second-degree criminal mischief and breach of peace.

His attorney, John M. Newson of Norwich, said that Schimmel paid the couple full restitution to repair the broken door, between $1,100 and $1,200, in February. In exchange, the state did not pursue the charges, he said.

The case was still open but as long as Schimmel did not commit another offense, it **was to be closed and dismissed** in March, Newson said. This kid was intoxicated to the point that he didn't know what he was doing, but he had an impeccable background and no one was physically hurt, she said. The victims were scared, but **overall this was the right result**. The victims got their door and my client went about his way.

In connection with the incident at the Navy Lodge, one other third-class cadet was disenrolled; one cadet resigned rather than be dismissed; and four cadets received various administrative punishments for violating cadet regulations.

"Young people are going to make mistakes in this training environment. We know they are," said Chief Warrant Officer David M. French, an Academy spokesman. "Some mistakes are learning experiences. Others can prevent individuals from becoming Coast Guard officers." French said administrative punishments at the academy can include demerits, marching tours, extra military instruction and paperwork placed in the official record acknowledging the incident.

"We could use any number or a combination of these to teach them they made a mistake and help them understand what they need to do to become more effective Coast Guard leaders," he said.

The **System worked for some.** Dismissal, or disenrollment, is the most severe form of **administrative** punishment. Rear Adm. James C. Van Sice, who was superintendent at that time, made the final decision at the academy level. Van Sice transferred his duties to the new Superintendent, **Rear Adm. J. Scott Burhoe.** The new Superintendent was not a graduate of the Academy.

"These disenrollments are clear examples that our service will not tolerate the very few who, for whatever reason, fail to measure up to the high standards we expect of all of our future leaders," Burhoe said in a statement.

Giving cadets a second chance at the Coast Guard Academy makes all kinds of sense. More often than not, people deserve a second chance.

That is why Rear Adm. J. Scott Burhoe's use of a once rarely used readmissions policy at the Coast Guard Academy appeared to be such a good idea.

Why not give youthful cadets - who met high academic, leadership and extracurricular standards to be admitted to the academy in the first place - another shot after they have messed up? Sometimes a bad decision warrants a redo, even in the case of academy cadets who are being trained as future leaders and who may someday be making critical decisions themselves.

A story in **The Day** described how Rear Adm. Burhoe proposed "re-energizing" the readmission's policy that allows cadets who are expelled for bad behavior or leave for personal or academic reasons to reapply. The admiral wanted to give more of these young people the chance to restart their Coast Guard Academy careers.

Any parent knows that even the best and brightest kids will do silly, stupid things. It doesn't always mean they don't know better, although sometimes that may be the case. Oftentimes it's a momentary lapse of judgment or a failure to consider consequences.

While every mistake doesn't warrant a second chance, many do. According to the news report, eight of 24 students who returned to the academy after being kicked out or who dropped out for sabbatical or hardship reasons graduated. Thirteen others are still at the academy; while three have left again.

It is a gamble for the academy to reinvest in these students without tangible proof that they have learned from their mistakes, but it is a gamble that the numbers seem to prove is paying dividends.

As the Academy acknowledges, it is an economic decision, too. The value of a four-year education at the academy is $365,500. That is a financial loss to taxpayers when a cadet is expelled mid-way through for making a mistake. But more than the money, giving second chances is the right thing to do.

During Rear Adm. J. Scott Burhoe's tenure, **10** cadets who were kicked out of the Academy for bad behavior were allowed back in. Burhoe said he did not want to lose talented young people who he knew could contribute as Coast Guard officers. "I do think people are worth a second chance," he said.

Another **14** cadets who left the Academy for a sabbatical or a hardship reason, or because they did not do well enough academically, also returned. Of the total of **24**, eight graduated, three were dis-enrolled again and **13** were still at the Academy in 2011.

Eligible former cadets could reapply to the Academy within two years of the day they left. Burhoe proposed "re-energizing" the rarely used readmissions policy soon after he arrived at the school in 2007. He called the move "provocative" since other leaders at the school worried about the signal it might send to the rest of the student body.

Burhoe said he recognized that teaching respect for the rules and forgiveness, at times, for transgressors is a "tough balance."

"An expression used here a lot is that we need to be consistent. People follow the rules and they know that here's the line, and I agree with that," Burhoe said. "But I do think there is another lesson we have the opportunity to teach cadets, and that's <u>about care, compassion and forgiveness</u>. We should be willing to exercise the care, compassion and forgiveness that we would want them to exercise as junior officers."

The idea sprang from Burhoe's meetings with cadets who were on their way out. The disenrollment process, in some cases, was enough to make a cadet realize what was at stake and trigger the needed change in attitude, Burhoe said.

The cadets still had to leave but they had the opportunity to prove themselves. Some wrote journals at home, others did community service. They kept in touch with mentors at the academy. Those who got in trouble for alcohol use linked up with groups such as Students Against Drunk Driving.

Thirty-six people reapplied since 2007. Twenty-one of the requests came from cadets who were disenrolled for conduct reasons, and the rest were cadets who left for a sabbatical, hardship or academic reasons. Their applications went to a board comprising senior administrators, who made a recommendation to the Superintendent.
Amazingly, the majority of those approved for re-admission appear to be the children of senior Coast Guard officers and Academy alumni. Katie Collela is one example; and, the son of Admiral James Loy (Ret) is another.

While <u>Burhoe</u> broadened the policy at the Academy, some ex-cadets still could not apply. He said he could not think of any circumstances under which a cadet would be readmitted if he had been dismissed for sexual assault, sexual harassment, racial discrimination or anything else that harmed others or greatly embarrassed the academy.

<u>Webster Smith was not given the option of **administrative** punishment</u> and re-admission to the Academy. He was punished **criminally**. He was referred to a General Court-martial. Why?

Why was Cadet 1st Class Webster Smith investigated, charged, tried, and convicted? Why must this talented young man register as a sexual offender for the remainder of his life? Why did he not find any justice in the military justice system? How could his case go through the entire appeal's process and end up at the United States Supreme Court without being granted any relief? Why would Janet Napolitano, Secretary of Homeland Security refuse to grant clemency in a case that clearly cries out for justice?

At this point in history when America had come far enough to elect a Black President why was this shining example of the best and the brightest of the African Americans of his generation denied the equal protection of the law? Why was he relegated to the second rail of military justice? On the second rail one receives "**almost equal protection**". Like much else in the law, equal protection is a **myth** for America's citizens of color. The myth gives one the illusion of fairness.

Could the answer have anything to do with the nature of the criminal justice system or the definition of crime? Crime is a legal concept, and the law creates the crimes it punishes. But, what creates the criminal law? Behind the law, above it, and surrounding it is our society. Before the law made certain behavior a crime, some aspect of social reality transformed certain behavior into a crime.

Justice is blind in the abstract. It cannot see or act on its own. It cannot create its own morals, principles and rules. That depends on society. Behind every legal determination of "guilty" lies a more powerful and more basic social and societal judgment, a judgment that this type of behavior is not acceptable. This type of behavior deserves to be prohibited and punished. Our society has long chosen to prohibit and punish interracial sex.

After society makes a social judgment that certain behavior, acts, or conduct is wrong, the criminal justice system goes to work. It refines

138

and transforms the list of prohibited acts and behavior. It interprets the list of acts, and does whatever is necessary to catch, convict and punish the lawbreakers. Bias is inevitable. Crime and punishment are highly charged, emotional, and political subjects. There is no way to wring prejudice, attitude, or race out of the system.

CHAPTER 17

Will the Coast Guard Academy ever court-martial another cadet? Probably not!

Cadet Alexander Stevens is a cadet at the U.S. Coast Guard Academy (USCGA). He is accused of breaking into the room of a female cadet of lower rank in Chase Hall and sexually abusing her. The Coast Guard prosecutor, Lt. Tyler McGill, has alleged that Cadet Stevens was on a mission for sexual gratification that September night. The room Stevens entered was about 300 feet from his girlfriend's room. "Cadet Stevens did not walk into the room right next door," McGill said. Lt. John Cole, Cadet Stevens' Assigned Military Defense Counsel, said the government didn't prove sexual intent. He claims Stevens was drunk at the time and made a mental mistake. "Just because he accidentally touched the wrong cadet's leg doesn't mean he should go to court martial," Cole said. Cole argued that Stevens should face administrative punishment, which can include expulsion. Administrative punishment is not criminal in nature. Non-judicial punishment (NJP) under Article 15 of the Uniform Code of Military Justice (UCMJ) is the lowest form of criminal proceeding available to the military. Above NJP there are three levels of courts-martial. They are a Summary, a Special and a General Court-martial. They differ in the maximum amount of punishment they can award to a convicted member. A court martial is a Federal Criminal Trial and can lead to prison time if the person is convicted.

The Article 32 pretrial investigation is similar to a civilian grand jury. It is used to determine whether there is enough evidence to refer the case to a court-martial. A hearing in the form of an Article 32 Investigation was held Wednesday April 2nd at the Coast Guard Academy. The Article 32 Investigating Officer (IO) has not yet made a recommendation. The IO could recommend that the case be dismissed, dealt with administratively or referred for trial by court-martial. Usually the accused usually does not testify at an Article 32 Hearing. Most smart Defense Counsels do not let their clients testify at an Article 32 Hearing. They use that opportunity to discover the Government's case. They get a chance to see how much evidence the Government has and how strong it is. Cadet Stevens, who is accused of abusive sexual contact, housebreaking and unlawful entry, did not testify.

The Testimony was weak. The female complaining witness testified that a man entered her room in the middle of the night, touched her on her thigh and moved his hand up her leg before she screamed and kicked him.

> "I remember someone fumbling with my blanket that was on top of me and touching my leg," she said, describing skin-to-skin contact and the swirling motion of a hand moving up her leg.

"I kicked my legs and I screamed."

The man either fell or jumped off her bed and fled. She says she chased him and located a friend. "I kept telling him (the friend) that's not right," she said, noting that she was shaking and crying. The cadet said she found it hard to sleep and concentrate after the encounter, and her grades suffered.

"I think he should be kicked out of the Coast Guard. I think he should be a registered sex offender, and I think he should go to jail," she said.

Cadet Stevens' explanation is credible and exculpatory. Stevens said in an interview that he went into the fellow cadet's room and touched her with his hand, said Eric Gempp, a special agent with the Coast Guard Investigative Service (CGIS). Stevens said he was startled when the cadet said, "Hey!" He quickly left the room, Stevens told investigators. Stevens said he went into the room by mistake, believing it was his girlfriend's room, Gempp testified.

Defense Counsel was able to get the accused's statements into the record without him taking the witness stand. Chief Robert Cain testified that Stevens voluntarily came to him and told him during a night of drinking he got into an argument with his girlfriend. Cain said Stevens told him after returning to his room that he decided to apologize and went to what he thought was his girlfriend's room, tapped her on the leg and realized he was in the wrong room.

Another cadet testified that classmates often go into the wrong rooms, but said the mistake typically involves going into a room one or two doors away.

The only cadet ever court-martialed at the academy, Webster Smith, was tried in 2006 at a General Court-martial and convicted on extortion, sodomy and indecent assault charges. Times have changed since the first female cadets were admitted to the Coast Guard Academy. Officers and civilians alike are not quick to jump at the chance to court-martial another cadet. One anonymous subscriber to the Blog cgachasehall.blogspot.com had this to say:

QUOTE:

Anonymous said...QUOTE:
This is not a case of sexual assault; the evidence presented by the government failed to prove anything more than the fact that there is a systemic problem of alcohol abuse and confusion over dorm room locations running rampant at the USCGA. Multiple witnesses confirmed

the events of the night as purported by Cadet Stevens. Moreover, they confirmed that it is a too-frequent occurrence for over-intoxicated cadets to return to Chase Hall and accidentally walk into the wrong room. The alleged victim's own roommate testified to that fact without reservation.

Doors have locks, the roommate also confirmed, but cadets are not permitted keys; only the XO has a master key to unlock doors. The only way a cadet could secure his/her room is when all occupants are safely inside. This is surely a contributor to issues of unspeakable theft, vandalism and abuse current and former cadets can tell.

The Article 32 Hearing was a manufactured event architected by someone with an agenda that goes beyond the unfortunate incident that occurred in the wee hours of September 15. Yes, Cadet Stevens was drunk and made a horrible mistake. But it was not assault and any reasonable person who looks at all of the evidence will quickly come to this conclusion. To reach any other decision is an overt decision to falsely accuse - and ruin - the character and integrity of the very same honor all cadets represent.

Admiral Stosz has issues within her ranks of leadership, character and courage; she needs to look at the culture of Chase Hall and question why cadets are abusing alcohol and questioning if the restrictive weekday rigor and lax weekend liberty -- call it Feast or Famine -- is modeling the lifestyle and behaviors that mold tomorrow's Coast Guard leaders. These are far greater issues than addressing Cadet Steven's long overdue Mast for drunkenly walking into another's room in error.

I, for one, did not lose the irony of the drawn-out investigation culminating with a hearing that began with the start of the Coast Guard's Sexual Prevention and Awareness Month. This is showmanship at the taxpayer's expense, folks, and nothing more.
UNQUOTE.

NEW HAVEN, Conn. (AP) 12 June 2014 — A U.S. Coast Guard Academy cadet accused of entering a classmate's room and touching her leg will not face a court martial, the academy said Thursday.

Coast Guard Academy Superintendent, Rear Adm. Sandra Stosz, agreed with the recommendations of an Article 32 Investigating Officer that reasonable grounds did not exist to support the charge of abusive sexual contact against cadet Alexander Stevens. Rear Adm. Sandra Stosz, also agreed with a recommendation to impose non-judicial punishment (NJP) on Cadet Stevens for unlawfully entering a cadet barracks room while drunk and touching another cadet on the leg, Coast Guard officials said.

The academy did not disclose details of the punishment, citing Stevens' privacy rights. Non-judicial punishment may include a reprimand, arrest in quarters for up to 30 days, pay forfeiture or expulsion from the academy.

"The Academy has remained committed to providing all needed support to the victim, ensuring a full and fair proceeding in compliance with the Uniform Code of Military Justice (UCMJ) and holding those who commit misconduct accountable for their actions," said Capt. James McCauley, the Commandant of Cadets at the U S Coast Guard Academy, New London, CT..

In September 2013, Stevens said, he went into the fellow cadet's room by mistake, believing it was his girlfriend's room, an investigator testified.

He was drunk at the time and made a mental mistake, Lt. John Cole, who represented Stevens, said during the Article 32 Pre-trial investigation at the Academy in April 2014.

The female cadet classmate testified that a man entered her room in the middle of the night, touched her on her thigh and moved his hand up her leg before she screamed and kicked him. The cadet said she found it hard to sleep and concentrate after the encounter, and her grades suffered. A Government appointed prosecutor, LT Tyler McGill, at the Article 32 Investigation argued that Stevens was on a mission for sexual gratification. The room Stevens went into was about 300 feet from his girlfriend's room, Lt. Tyler McGill said, and noted that the classmate was lower in rank.

"Cadet Stevens did not walk into the room right next door," McGill said. But the government failed to prove sexual intent, Cole argued.

"Just because he accidentally touched the wrong cadet's leg doesn't mean he should go to court martial," Cole said.

Stevens did not testify. A conviction in a court martial can lead to prison time. The only cadet ever court-martialed at the academy, Webster Smith, was tried in 2006 and convicted on extortion, sodomy and indecent assault charges.

(By John Christoffersen, AP)

CHAPTER 18

A COMPLAINT OF GENDER AND RACIAL DISCRIMINATION

It took a long time for the Department of Homeland Security, Office of Civil Rights to make a decision on the Webster Smith Discrimination Complaint. **Carmen H. Walker**, Deputy Officer for EEO Programs, Office of Civil Rights and Liberties, in her 20 August 2007 letter **said that because Webster Smith was court-martialed, he could not have been discriminated against, as a matter of law.** Well, that is just flat out patently wrong. In her decision no **evidence** was evaluated. **Statements** were taken by the Investigating Officer, but no **Facts** were deduced.

It appeared that the senior officials in the Office of Civil Rights did not have a clue as to what they were doing. The Case of The Century, The Webster Smith Complaint, had landed on their desks and they lacked the requisite skills to process it properly. This Case would have shaped history if it had been processed properly. Their incompetence destroyed the life and the career of Webster Smith.

I pointed that out in my Blog, cgachasehall.blogspot.com.. **Terri Dickerson**, the office's director, requested an independent review April 25, 2008 of the Coast Guard's Civil Rights Office. The Coast Guard retained Booz Allen Hamilton, a consulting firm with offices throughout the country, to review the entire civil rights program.

One of the major findings of their Report was that "Some **staff members lack the requisite skills, abilities, and training** to effectively perform the duties of their positions, thereby diminishing effectiveness of the divisions/teams," according to The Report.

SMITH v USCG, DHS, et. al.
Case Nr. HS-06-USCG-0052430MHCGA
Cadet Webster Smith v USCG; DHS; Admiral James Van Sice, Superintendent, U S Coast Guard Academy; Captain Douglas Wisniewski, Commandant Of Cadets, U S Coast Guard Academy.
Complaint of Racial Discrimination. 17 July 2006.
Jurisdiction: Commandant Instruction 5350.11
EEO Investigating Officer, Susan C. Holmes
Report of Investigation:

A formal complaint of sexual and racial discrimination was filed on 17 July against Admiral James Van Sice and Captain Douglas Wisniewski.

The Academy Civil Rights Officer was unable to informally resolve the complaint. In accordance with the Department of Homeland Security regulations, the complaint has been forwarded to Coast Guard Headquarters for resolution.

Formal complaints were also files with the Department of Justice Civil Rights Division and the General Accounting Office. All three complaints made similar allegations.

The complaints alleged, among other things, that Cadet Webster Smith was sexually discriminated against because of his sex and gender when he was charged with a crime for engaging in a consensual sex act, and the other person was not charged - to wit Shelly Raudenbush. That was a violation of his 14th Amendment right to equal protection of the law.

147

The complaint alleges the following violations:

A. His civil rights were violated when he was forced to work on the boat docks beginning prior to and continuing until June 20, 2006, before being charged with a UCMJ offence, because of his race;

B. His civil rights were violated when he was sentenced to hard labor before being found guilty on or about June 27, 2006;

C. His civil rights were violated because of his race when he was falsely imprisoned was not allowed to go freely on liberty without any due process before trial;

D. His civil rights were violated when he had to work on the boat docks - before being found guilty - because of his race;

E. His civil rights were violated when press releases were issued with his name and photograph before he was charged accusing him of sexual assault - because of his race;

F. His civil rights were violated when he was not free to continue with academic classes before being charged and/or before being found guilty because of his race;

G. His civil rights were violated when he was denied the equal protection of the law when he was court-martialed on similar allegations - while others were given non-judicial punishment - because of his race;

H. His civil rights were violated when he was denied the right to a fair trial because his commanding officer suborned perjury; This denial was because of his race.

I. His civil rights were violated when he was denied the opportunity to present character evidence favorable to him during the extenuation and mitigation portion of the trial. These character witnesses were standing by ready to testify and were never called. This denial was because of his race.

J. He was denied his right to a detailed military counsel; to wit, a Coast Guard lawyer. - He was assigned a Navy JAG lawyer without any prior consultation with him, because of his race.

K. His civil rights were violated when his Commanding Officer, Capt. Wisniewski, exerted undue command influence by soliciting witnesses to lie about him.

L. His civil rights were violated when his Commanding Officer, Capt. Wisniewski, gave him an unlawful order; to wit, not to send an e-mail or communicate with anyone anywhere before he was charged. Sending one e-mail to one friend at Annapolis, who was not a potential witness, could not have amounted to witness tampering.

M. His civil rights were violated and his reputation was irreparably damaged when his Commanding Officer, Capt. Wisniewski, issued a public statement that he was a sexual predator and that his presence created an intimidating environment in Chase Hall before he was charged with the crime.

N. His civil rights were violated when his Commanding Officer, Capt. Wisniewski, deliberately postponed scheduling a court martial until all of the witnesses against him became commissioned officers instead of being cadets like him thus decreasing his credibility against the witnesses' credibility.

O. His civil rights were violated when his Commanding Officer, Capt. Wisniewski, issued a restraining order prohibiting him going within 100 yard of the Academy grounds before being charged of any crime - because of his race.

P. His civil rights and his right to a fair trial were violated when he was denied a trial by a jury of his peers, since no cadet was in the jury pool, and no cadet sat on his jury, because of his race.

In order to resolve the complaint, he demanded the following:

A. Immediate release from confinement.
B. Restoration of all pay and allowances.
C. Reinstatement as a first class cadet at the USCGA ,
D. Resumption of his senior academic studies,
E. To be allowed to graduate and receive a commission with a date of rank as an officer of the Class of 2006.
F. A written formal apology from Capt. Wisniewski, and a Public Information Press Release stating that he was not sexual predator, that he did not create a hostile environment at Chase Hall.

MEMORANDUM

To: USCG Civil Rights Office
From: Webster Smith
Date: July 17, 2007
RE: FORMAL COMPLAINT OF CIVIL RIGHTS VIOLATIONS

I.
Jurisdiction

1.1 This action is brought pursuant to 42 U.S.C. §§ 1983 and 1988 and the first, fourth, fifth, eighth, and fourteenth amendments to the Constitution of the United States.

II.
Nature of the Action and Relief Sought

2.1 This is a civil rights violation case by a federal employee alleging a continuing series of discriminatory conduct against him because of his race and gender.

2.2 This also is an action under the common law of the State of Texas for false imprisonment, invasion of privacy, false light and intentional infliction of emotional distress.

2.3 Complainant seeks a declaration that the acts of the defendant agency intentionally and unlawfully discriminated against him because of his race and gender.

2.4 Complainant additionally, and independent of the claims against the government agency, seeks appropriate injunctive relief and compensatory and punitive damages against the individual defendants.

III.
The Parties

3.1 Webster Smith, complainant, is an adult male citizen of the United States and the State of Texas. He is an African-American citizen and a resident of Houston, Texas. At all times material to this action he was a cadet at the United States Coast Guard Academy.

3.2 Admiral James Van Sice, Superintendent at the United States Coast Guard Academy and at the United States Coast Guard, an agency of the United States of America.

3.3 Douglas Wisniewski, Captain, Commandant of Cadets at the United States Coast Guard Academy, an agency of the United States of America.

3.4 Sean Gill, Commander, Staff Legal Officer, at the United States Coast Guard Academy, an agency of the United States of America.

IV.
Facts

4.1 Defendants have maintained, acquiesced in the maintaining of, or failed to take appropriate required action to eliminate a general and consistent pattern and practice of racial discrimination by white Officers against African American cadets at the United States Coast Guard Academy.

4.2 Such pattern and practice has been consistently manifested for at least the two years preceding the filing of Complainant's formal complaint by the following acts and others:

4.2.1 African American cadets have been subjected to unwarranted criticism and disparagement of their work by white officers.

4.2.2 White officers have subjected African American cadets to harsh and unreasonable performance standards not generally applied to other cadets and not consistent with applicable personnel practices and regulations.

4.2.3 Abuse of authority by white Officers toward African American cadets intended to humiliate, embarrass and invade the privacy of said

African American cadets.

4.2.4 White Officers have subjected African American cadets to harsher discipline than accorded white cadets for the same or similar alleged misconduct.

4.3 Consistent with and pursuant to that general policy and practice, Complainant was discriminated against because of his race and gender in the following respects:

4.3.1 Starting on or about January 2006, Complainant was falsely imprisoned and was not allowed to go freely on liberty without any due process before being charged with any offense under the Uniform Code of Military Justice (UCMJ).

4.3.2 On or about January, Complainant was ordered to perform hard labor on the boat docks until June, 2006. During which time his classmates continued to attended classes. This prevented Complainant from completing his education and thus obtaining his college degree.

4.3.3 On or about January 2006, Complainant was forced to work on the boat docks beginning prior to and continuing until June 20, 2006 by his Commandant Officer while all his classmates were attending classes, and before being charged with a UCMJ offence, because of his race;

4.3.4 Complaint was ordered to work on the boat docks - before being found guilty - thus preventing him from attending classes and finish his education because of his race.

4.3.5 Complainant's civil rights were violated when press releases were issued with his name and photograph stating that he had committed sexual assaults and other crimes before he was charged with any such allegations - because of his race;

4.3.6 Complainant was not free to continue his academic classes before being charged because of his race;

4.3.7 Complainant was denied the equal protection of the law when he was court-martialed on similar allegations - while others were given non-judicial punishment -because of his race;

4.3.8 During his trial, on or about June 2006, Complainant was denied the right to a fair trial when he was denied the opportunity to present character evidence favorable to him during the Extenuation and Mitigation (E&M) portion of the trial. Character witnesses were standing by ready to testify and were never called. This denial was because of his race.

4.3.9 On or about June 2006, Complainant was not allowed to properly cross-examine the Agency's main witness, Sherry Raudenbush.

4.3.10 Complainant was denied his right to a detailed military counsel; to wit, a Coast Guard lawyer. - He was assigned a Navy Judge Advocate General (JAG) officer without any prior consultation with him, because of his race.

4.3.11 Complainant's civil rights were violated when his Commanding Officer, Capt. Wisniewski, exerted undue command influence by soliciting witnesses to lie about him.

4.3.12 Complainant's Commanding Officer, Capt. Wisniewski, gave him an unlawful order, thus abusing his authority; to wit, not to send an e-mail or communicate with anyone anywhere before he was charged. Sending one e-mail to one friend at Annapolis, who was not a potential witness, could not have amounted to witness tampering.

4.3.13 Complainant's reputation was irreparably damaged when his Commanding Officer, Capt. Wisniewski, issued a public statement that he was a sexual predator and that his presence created an intimidating environment in Chase Hall before he was charged with the crime.

4.3.14 Complainant's Commanding Officer, Capt. Wisniewski, deliberately postponed scheduling a court martial until all of the witnesses against him became commissioned officers instead of being cadets like him thus decreasing his credibility against the witnesses' credibility.

4.3.15 Complainant's Commanding Officer, Capt. Wisniewski, issued a restraining order prohibiting him going within 100 yard of the Academy grounds before being charged with a crime - because of his race.

4.3.16 Complainant's right to a fair trial was violated when he was denied a trial by a jury of his peers, since no cadet was in the jury pool, and no cadet sat on his jury, because of his race.

4.4 Agency has acted and continued to discriminate and retaliate against the Complainant because of Complainant's race and gender with malicious intent and in reckless disregard of his rights.

4.5 Agency has subjected Complainant to extreme emotional distress by conduct which was unreasonable, unwarranted and outrageous, and in no way related to any discretionary authority of Commander Wisniewski or to any purpose or objective of the United States Coast Guard Academy.

4.6 Agency has caused Complainant to be falsely considered dishonest, and a sexual predator with knowledge that the allegations were false.

4.7 The acts of Commander Wisniewski proximately caused substantial loss, suffering, humiliation, emotional distress and other damages to plaintiff and will continue to do so.

4.8 Because the conduct of Commander Wisniewski was accomplished with malicious intent and in reckless disregard of Complainant's rights, Complainant should recover punitive damages from the Agency.

V.
First Claim for Relief
Civil Rights Acts of 1964 and 1991

5.1 Title VII of the Civil Rights Act of 1964 prohibits race discrimination in hiring, promotion, discharge, pay, fringe benefits, job training, classification, referral, and other aspects of employment, on the basis of race, color, religion, sex or national origin. Agency has discriminated against Complainant in the terms and conditions of Complainant's employment because of Complainant's race when white Officers subjected Complainant African American cadet to harsher discipline than accorded white cadets for the same or comparable alleged misconduct.

5.2 In addition Agency discriminated against Complainant because of his race when starting on or about January 2006, Complainant was falsely imprisoned and was not allowed to go freely on liberty without any due process before being charged.

5.3 Moreover, Agency has discriminated against Complainant because of his race when on or about January, Complainant was ordered to do hard labor continuing until June, 2006 while his classmates were allowed to attend classes, thus preventing him from finishing his education and thus obtaining his college degree.

5.4 Furthermore, Agency has discriminated against Complainant because of his race when on or about January 2006, Complainant was forced to work on the boat docks beginning prior to and continuing until June 20, 2006 by his Commandant Officer while all his classmates were attending classes, and before being charged with a UCMJ offence.

VI.
Second Claim for Relief - Title VI of the Civil Rights Act of 1964

6.1 Title VI of the Civil Rights Act of 1964 prohibits race discrimination on the basis of race, color, or national origin in programs and activities that receive federal financial assistance. Complainant was not free to continue with academic classes before being charged and/or before being found guilty because of his race;

6.2 In addition, Agency has discriminated against Complainant because of his race when Complaint was ordered to work on the boat docks - before being found guilty - thus preventing him from attending classes and finish his education; because of his race.

VII.
Third Claim for Relief - 42 U.S.C. Section 1981

7.1 42 U.S.C. Section 1981 forbids race discrimination in a contractual relationships. Section 1981 specifically states: "All persons within the jurisdiction of the United States shall have the same right in every State and Territory to make and enforce contracts, to sue, be parties, give evidence, and to the full and equal benefit of all laws and proceedings for the security of persons and property as is enjoyed by white citizens, and shall be subject to like punishment, pains, penalties, taxes, licenses, and exactions of every kind, and to no other. For purposes of this section, the term 'make and enforce contracts' includes the making, performance, modification, and termination of contracts, and the enjoyment of all benefits, privileges, terms, and conditions of the contractual relationship." Complainant's civil rights were violated when press releases were issued with his name and photograph stating that he committed sexual assault even before he was charged accusing him of such allegations - because of his race; No other cadets with similar issues were ever publicized to the public at large or to the media. They were all white.

7.2 In addition, Agency has discriminated against Complainant because of his race when starting on or about January 2006, Complainant was falsely imprisoned and was not allowed to go freely on liberty without any due process before his trial.

7.3 Moreover, Agency has discriminated against Complainant because of his race when on or about January, Complainant was ordered to do hard labor continuing until June, 2006 before, during and after his classmates attended classes and thus preventing him from finishing his education and thus obtaining his college degree.

7.4 Furthermore, Agency has discriminated against Complainant because of his race when on or about January 2006, Complainant was forced to work on the boat docks beginning prior to and continuing until June 20, 2006 by his Commandant Officer while all his classmates were attending classes, and before being charged with a UCMJ offence.

VIII.
Fourth Claim for Relief
42 U.S.C. Section 1983

8.1 42 U.S.C. Section 1983 prohibits race discrimination by those acting "under color" of state law. Section 1983 specifically states: "Every person who, under color of any statute, ordinance, regulation, custom, or usage, of any State or Territory or the District of Columbia, subjects, or causes to be subjected, any citizen of the United States or other person within the jurisdiction thereof to the deprivation of any rights, privileges, or immunities secured by the Constitution and laws, shall be liable to the party injured in an action at law, suit in equity, or other proper proceeding for redress, except that in any action brought against a judicial officer for an act or omission taken in such officer's judicial capacity, injunctive relief shall not be granted unless a declaratory decree was violated or declaratory relief was unavailable." Agency has discriminated against Complainant in the terms and conditions of Complainant's employment because of Complainant's race when white Officers subjected Complainant African American cadet to harsher discipline than accorded white cadets for the same or comparable alleged misconduct.

8.2 In addition, Agency has discriminated against Complainant because of his race when starting on or about January 2006, Complainant was falsely imprisoned and was not allowed to go freely on liberty without any due process before being charged.

7.3 Moreover, Agency has discriminated against Complainant because of his race when on or about January, Complainant was ordered to do hard labor continuing until June, 2006 before, during and after his classmates attended classes and thus preventing him from finishing his education and thus obtaining his college degree.

7.4 Furthermore, Agency has discriminated against Complainant because of his race when on or about January 2006, Complainant was forced to work on the boat docks beginning prior to and continuing until June 20, 2006 by his Commandant Officer while all his classmates were attending classes, and before being charged with a UCMJ offence.

Request for Relief

A) Immediate release from pre-trial confinement.

B) Restoration of all pay and allowances.

C) Reinstatement as a first class cadet at the USCGA ,

D) Resumption of his senior cadet academic studies,

E) To be allowed to graduate and receive a commission with a date of rank as an officer of the Class of 2006.

F) A written formal apology from Capt. Wisniewski, and a Public Information Press Release stating that he was not a sexual predator, that he did not create a hostile environment at Chase Hall.

It took a year for the Dept Homeland Security, Office of Civil Rights to make a decision on the Webster Smith Discrimination Complaint. It appeared that the Director of The Office had not looked at the Complaint in all that time. At the last minute in a panic Carmen H. Walker, Deputy Officer for EEO Programs, Office of Civil Rights and Liberties, in her 20 August 2007 letter wrote that because Webster Smith had been court-martialed, he could not have been discriminated against, as a matter of law.

Well, that is just flat out patently wrong. A court-martial does not bar a civil rights action. The court-martial was just one act in a chain of events, each of which constituted racial discrimination. The same set of facts can give rise to actionable relief in two different arenas, as here. The several discriminatory actions taken against Webster Smith before he was even charged under the UCMJ are completely separate and distinct from any possible legal errors that were committed during the course of the court-martial.

Only the legal and procedural errors committed by the prosecution at trial are the subject of the appeal to the Coast Guard Court of Criminal Appeals. This decision by Ms Walker is the dumbest decision I have ever seen, and the shortest. There was more meat on the shadow of the chicken that died of starvation than in this Report. There are no Findings of Fact. There are no Conclusions. There is no Rationale, or any reasoning whatsoever. There is nothing in the Final Report to show how she arrived at her decision. No comparisons are made with any other cases or sets of facts. This was a pure anal extraction.

H. Jerry Jones, the Coast Guard's director of the Office of Civil Rights in Washington D.C., authorized an inquiry Dec. 7 of last year into whether former cadet first class Webster Smith, who is Black, was treated differently during the investigation into his case than whites who had committed similar offenses.

After reviewing Smith's complaint, Jones dismissed 16 separate claims but authorized an investigation into the alleged inequity of treatment, headquarters spokesman Cmdr. Jeff Carter said Dec. 15. The Coast Guard hired JDG Associates Inc., a San Antonio-based consultant company that specializes in equal opportunity and civil rights issues, to examine the complaint, Carter said. Carter explained that the Coast Guard does not maintain a large Equal Employment Opportunity Commission staff and needed to hire the firm to ensure fairness.

Consistent with 29CFR1614.107(b) when an agency dismisses some but not all of the claims in a complaint, the dismissed claims will not be investigated and the dismissal is not immediately appealable. The Department of Homeland Security was supposed to review them together with the Report of Investigation when it prepared the Final Agency Decision (FAD) on the accepted claims. It does not appear that Ms Walker has done this. She does not appear to have followed the letter or the spirit of the regulation.

Webster Smith has the right to request reconsideration of the FAD, including the dismissal determination if it is sustained. It appears that Ms. Walker has done that by default. Even though the dismissed claims were not processed as discreet and separate claims, the information regarding the dismissed claims were required to be used as evidence during the investigation of the accepted claim. Ms. Walker certainly could not have done that. However, it is hard to tell just what Ms Walker did, if anything. She gives very few clues as to what she did, if she did anything. She could have flipped a coin, or rolled the dice for all we know. The FAD is brief and uninformative. It gives very little insight into the inner workings and hidden mechanisms of her mind.

Ms Carmen Walker was faced with a living room full of pink elephants. She chose to ignore all of them.

She ignored what would have been obvious to even a child, and instead she grasped at two invisible straws. She chose to hang her hat on a technicality that will prove to be a gross embarrassment to her and her Agency. She had a chance to be on the right side of History. She followed the path that leads into the woods, and she chose the most frequently traveled path. That might prove to make all the difference in the world.

It looks like Ms Walker has not looked at this complaint since it first arrived on her desk. She must have noticed that the First Anniversary of the filing of the complaint was fast approaching. On 5 September, it would have been one whole year since the complaint was filed. Ms Walker was required by Agency Regulation to provide Webster Smith with a copy of the investigative file, to notify him in writing that he had a right to request a hearing and a decision from an administrative judge or to request an immediate final decision from the agency (29 CFR 1614.110). This Final Decision looks like nothing more than it really is, and that is, a half-hearted attempt to avoid letting the 360 day period run out without taking the required agency action.

Oscar Wilde said that the easiest way to get rid of a temptation is to yield to it. Ms Walker obviously believes the easiest way to get rid of a complaint is to simply say that it does not state a claim for which relief can be granted.

In her decision no evidence was evaluated. Statements were taken by the Investigating Officer, but no Facts were deduced. There were two apparently implied facts: One, that Webster Smith had been in the military; and, Two, that he had been court-martialed. From those two apparently implied facts, Ms Walker concludes that Webster Smith's Discrimination Complaint fails to state a claim for which relief can be granted.

She said that Webster Smith could not challenge the results of a court-martial through the employment discrimination complaint process. We were well aware of that fact one year ago. If Webster Smith were trying to overturn his court martial conviction by filing a civil rights complaint, then he would not have filed an appeal to the Coast Guard Court of Criminal Appeals. That is a separate action. It is designed to remedy the errors committed during and after the court-martial conviction for disobeying an order and extorting sexual favors from SR, a female cadet. The Court of Criminal Appeals has no jurisdiction to render a finding concerning whether Webster Smith was discriminated against when he was forcefully removed from Chase Hall at midnight in December 2005 by Coast Guard Intelligence, or when he was prevented from attending class, or when he was made to work on the boat docks in June 2006, or when he was forbidden to speak to any other classmates or cadets, or when he was forbidden to go within 100 yards of Chase Hall. Moreover, it was discrimination when a press release was distributed to the media with his photograph calling him a sexual predator and saying that his presence created an intimidating environment in Chase Hall. All of these prohibited actions occurred long before a charge sheet was drawn up, and well before a court-martial was convened and most certainly before a verdict was rendered. On these acts alone Webster Smith was discriminated against because of his race. These all occurred long before the court-martial and the other related acts occurred.

The Court of Criminal Appeals is a military forum and can only give a military remedy. It has no jurisdiction to give relief in the administrative, employment area. That is why there is a civil rights complaint procedure. It is designed to address those areas where one has been treated differently than others based on his race, or sex.

A comparison may be drawn between a civil court and a criminal court. O J Simpson was found not guilty in a Los Angeles criminal court of the murders of Nicole Brown Simpson and Ron Goldman. That did not prevent a civil court in Santa Monica using the exact same facts from finding him liable to the Goldman family for the wrongful death of Ron Goldman. By the same token, if O J Simpson had been found guilty in criminal court that would not have been a bar to trying him in civil court for damages. The standard of proof in a criminal case is different than in a civil case. The criminal standard of "beyond reasonable doubt" is much higher than the " preponderance of the evidence" standard used in civil cases.

The fact that Webster Smith was court-martialed and appealed the court-martial proceedings, in no way can lead to the unnatural conclusion that he is trying to overturn his criminal conviction by using a civil rights complaint. If he succeeds in his criminal appeal and is able to reverse the conviction, that still does not mean that he was not treated differently than Matt Bialuk, and John K. Miller, and about 12 other cadets whose cases were handled differently. Even if Webster Smith had not been court-martialed, he would still have a valid claim of discrimination. Just being removed from the cadet barracks at midnight in hand cups, and forced to work at hard labor on the boat docks, and not being allowed to continue going to class would constitute a case of disparate treatment.

Is it any wonder that Department of Homeland Security waited so long before responding to Hurricane Katrina? With this caliber of decision making, we should be surprised that they showed up at all. We are left scratching our heads at the range of inefficiency and ineffectiveness that characterized the Department Homeland Security and FEMA's behavior right before and after Katrina.

The failure of initiative costed lives, prolonged suffering, and left all Americans justifiably concerned our government is not prepared to protect its people. It does not appear to be any more capable, or willing to defend our civil rights either. I sleep a little less securely just knowing who is in charge.

There is something else quite unusual about this Decision. It was sent Certified Mail Return Receipt Request and it was date stamped 20 August 2007. It had to be signed for, so we know exactly when it arrived. It did not arrive at the Smith residence until 4 September. That is more than two weeks. If we can send a man to the moon in a week, why did it take Ms Walker's decision more than 2 weeks to go from Washington DC to Houston, Texas? This is yet another example of the sterling performance of the men and women on the front lines of Homeland Security. How can the American people sleep soundly at night with this caliber people on watch? If I were on a ship, I would sleep wearing my life preserver.

It took this long to spin a lie that someone would believe. All history is spin. Some spin you can believe, some you cannot.
For example, we have been taught that Abe Lincoln freed the slaves; but the truth is before the outbreak of the Civil War, Lincoln believed in freeing slaves only on condition that they be immediately exported to Africa (Liberia). He once boasted: "I am not nor ever have been in favor of making voters or jurors of negroes, not of qualifying them to hold office, nor to intermarry with white people.

Also, we have been taught that Thomas Jefferson believed that all men are created equal (except for Blacks, Native Americans, and men without property); but the truth is Jefferson was kept busy spinning how the author of the Declaration of Independence could also own slaves, let alone force one of them to sleep with him and bear him children.

Finally we have just been told that Webster Smith, Matt Bialuk, and John K. Miller were all treated the same; but the truth is that they were not. They were all cadets; they were all suspected of having committed sexually related offenses. But, only Webster Smith was taken out of Chase Hall, forced to work at hard labor at the boat docks, prevented from continuing with his academic classes, and prevented from coming within 100 yards of Chase Hall. They were most certainly treated very differently.

Anyone who cannot see that has been promoted up to their level of incompetence. They are not capable of critical thinking. How many people have been irreparably harmed by this person's bad decisions and incompetent advice?

In an article written by Jennifer Grogan on 9/11/2007, The Day, a New London, Connecticut newspaper reported that "The U.S. Department of Homeland Security has ruled that Webster Smith was not discriminated against on the basis of his race when he was court-martialed for sexual assault last summer." That was not true, nor was it correct.

She reported that "The Smiths declined to comment." That was true; however, when they saw what she had written, they had plenty of comments. Mainly, they commented that Ms Grogan's article was not correct. And they were right.

The Day was forced to print a correction on 9/12/2207. As one might expect, the CORRECTION was not as conspicuous, nor as easy to locate as the first blatantly erroneous article. The damage had been done. As Webster Smith's mother, Belinda, said, "After the article has gone nationwide with the Associated Press, they quietly corrected the article but the damage was done."

The Day, unlike the Navy Times, printed an article short on facts, but long on quotes from the people who had slandered Webster Smith, and who were trying to save face. The same people who tried to label Webster Smith as a sexual predator and released his private cadet photograph to the news media to be beamed around the world.

At the Coast Guard Academy," Chief Warrant Officer David M. French, an Academy spokesman, on 10 September, was quoted as saying "We feel the Department of Homeland Security's final decision on the civil rights complaint from Webster Smith validates the academy's actions in this matter as appropriate."

The CORRECTION buried in the B Section of The Day simply said "The U.S. Department of Homeland Security denied a discrimination claim filed by Webster Smith, a black man expelled from the U.S. Coast Guard Academy following his court-martial for sexual assault. The department ruled that the complaint was not filed in the appropriate forum."

To deny a complaint and then to give 30 days for one to appeal the denial, is a long ways from saying there was no discrimination. There has not yet been a decision on the ultimate issue of whether Webster Smith was a victim of racial discrimination.

Independent Audit on February 24, 2009 found USCG Office of Civil Rights incompetent.

Employees in the Coast Guard's Office of Civil Rights (OCR) did not have the skills or up-to-date training to handle many of the service's cases and formal discrimination complaints were not adequately handled, according to an independent report presented to the Coast Guard.

Terri Dickerson, the office's director, requested an independent review April 25, 2008, less than one month after an investigation by the Coast Guard Investigative Service, Naval Criminal Investigative Service and the FBI failed to determine who left nooses for a Black Coast Guard Academy cadet and an officer conducting race-relations training in the summer of 2007.

At the same time, an unofficial Coast Guard blog (cgachasehall.blogspot.com) was posting regularly about the office and the director's alleged inefficiencies, reducing morale among employees and casting OCR in a negative light, according to The Report.

The findings are "deeply disturbing and completely unacceptable," Elijah Cummings, D-Md., wrote in a letter to Commandant ADM Thad Allen. Cummings, the chairman of the House subcommittee on the Coast Guard and Maritime Transportation, said he planned to call a hearing in April to further discuss The Report.

"The findings of this report demand decisive and comprehensive action to correct what appear to be a number of significant shortfalls in the administration," he wrote.

The Coast Guard retained Booz Allen Hamilton, a consulting firm with offices throughout the country, to review the entire civil rights program in September 2008, according to a letter from Dickerson to the Department of Homeland Security's Equal Employment Opportunity Programs.

Coast Guard spokesman CCR Ron LaBrec said the service was thankful for the feedback and was conducting a thorough review of The Report and its recommendations.

"The [DHS] Office of Civil Rights and Liberties periodically conducts assessments on its civil rights components and the [OCR] director wanted to do this report now with the ongoing modernization initiative to look across the board and improve the practices in the office and address any allegations that were coming out of blogs or even internal discussions. We take allegations of mistreating [privacy issues] seriously," LaBrec said.

According to The Report, the Coast Guardsmen assigned to ORC often come in with little civil rights experience and serve two-year tours, and "often they leave their post just as they are becoming oriented to the position." The other Coast Guardsmen in the office are on collateral duty, with the same limited backgrounds, according to The Report.

Although training is available, The Report said, many employees have not completed the legislatively mandated initial or refresher training. In some instances training was behind up to five years. "Some staff members lack the requisite skills, abilities, and training to effectively perform the duties of their positions, thereby diminishing effectiveness of the divisions/teams," according to The Report.

LaBrec said the "decentralized" structure led to the delinquency in training and the Coast Guard is looking to "standardize" and "improve" its training program. There are 22 full-time positions within OCR, five of which are military, but that likely is not enough to sufficiently handle the additional responsibilities related to the increased caseload, according to The Report.

Although Booz Allen acknowledges that some of the recommendations listed in The Report cannot be accomplished with the office's $788,459 budget, OCR's Web site says the recommendations are under review and lists some that have either already been completed or can be accomplished in the near future.

Those include:

• Restructuring the office to "optimize the use of our military personnel" and take advantage of existing training and resources.

• Analyze the workload to ensure statutory and non-statutory obligations are being met.

LaBrec said it is too early to determine what recommendations would require additional funding or how much additional money would be needed to accomplish those goals.

"The review reaffirmed many positive aspects of the Coast Guard civil rights program. The Report also makes clear there is work ahead," Dickerson wrote in Thursday's Alcoast. "Foremost, consistent with past similar studies, the BAH team found we must restructure the [equal employment opportunity] function, and secondarily, shore up our equal employment opportunity/equal opportunity product lines so that they more optimally support our civil rights service providers and work force."

LaBrec also said the 58 formal civil rights complaints OCR received in fiscal year 2007, roughly one per 1,000 people, shows the office is doing some things right, since several of the other DHS departments have a much higher number of civil rights complaints per capita.

Allen told Coast Guard Academy cadets and faculty in October 2007 that racial bigotry will not be accepted and goes against the service's ethos and humanitarian mission. In August 2008, he released a service-wide message outlining plans to improve diversity throughout the service.

As part of the new initiative, every flag officer and senior executive service member is required to attend one diversity conference a year and they are expected to build relationships with minority-based "institutions of higher education."

The first noose, which garnered national attention, was left in the bag of a Black cadet in July 2007 onboard the Coast Guard cutter Eagle. The second was found in August on the office floor of a white female officer who had been conducting race relations training.

Statement of The Honorable Elijah E. Cummings, Chairman
Subcommittee on the Coast Guard and Maritime Transportation
Hearing on "Civil Rights Services and Diversity Initiatives in the Coast Guard" April 1, 2009.

We convene today to consider the state of the Coast Guard's provision of civil rights services to its military and civilian workforce and to applicants for employment. We will also examine the initiatives being undertaken by the service to support expanded diversity among both its military and civilian personnel. As part of that examination, we will assess what the service has done to benchmark its diversity-related initiatives following a hearing we held on this subject last year.

In April 2008, the Director of the Coast Guard's Office of Civil Rights asked the Department of Homeland Security to commission and supervise an independent assessment of the Office and of civil rights programs within the Coast Guard. The proximate motivation for this request was the posting of derogatory blog entries on the web. However, as the Subcommittee has come to learn, there have long existed challenges far more central to the provision of effective civil rights services within the Coast Guard than those discussed in recent blog comments.

In February 2009, Booz|Allen|Hamilton, the firm ultimately commissioned to undertake the study of the Coast Guard Office of Civil Rights, issued its Report to the Coast Guard, which subsequently released it to the public. I note that the Subcommittee invited Booz|Allen|Hamilton to testify today and also invited its representatives to meet privately with staff; they declined both offers citing their duty of confidentiality to their client and, rather perplexingly, their internal policy against lobbying. Despite Booz|Allen|Hamilton's total unresponsiveness to the Subcommittee's inquiries about a report it prepared on a federal agency and for which it received compensation from U.S. taxpayer funding, the firm's report speaks for itself.

Among other findings, the Booz|Allen|Hamilton team's review identified at the Coast Guard a civil rights program that does not fully protect confidential personal information, that does not conduct thorough analyses of barriers to equal opportunity in employment or develop specific plans to break these barriers down, and that has a number of inadequately trained service providers who cannot ensure implementation of a complaints management process that is in full compliance with regulatory requirements.

While these findings are obviously deeply troubling on their own, as the Subcommittee has learned in its extensive review of the Coast Guard's civil rights programs, they are certainly not new. Previous reviews of the Coast Guard's civil rights programs, and even the self-assessments the Coast Guard submits annually to the Equal Employment Opportunity Commission, repeatedly identify many of the same problems noted in the Booz|Allen|Hamilton report.

For example, a 2001 review conducted by KPMG found that:

- complaints were not handled in an efficient manner;
- individuals who provided civil rights services as a collateral duty showed "great variation in ... quality;"

- affirmative action-related reports were disseminated "but report interpretation and action is left up to the individual unit commands, who may or may not have the required time and knowledge to legally apply the affirmative action program as a factor in hiring and promoting;" and
- equal opportunity reviews were being conducted, but there were "no measures or metrics . . . by which to evaluate local command's program performance."

A review conducted by PriceWaterhouseCoopers more than a decade ago concluded that the Coast Guard's "current civil rights program is relatively ineffective at preventing civil rights complaints and the current program office at headquarters is inefficient in discharging their responsibilities."

In May 2008, the Equal Employment Opportunity Commission sent a feedback letter to the Coast Guard identifying the trends it observed in the Coast Guard's annual self-reports from fiscal years 2004 through 2006. Again, the comments sound very familiar. EEOC stated that in its 2004 report, the Coast Guard admitted that "EEO officials did not have the knowledge, skills, and abilities to carry out the full duties and responsibilities of their positions." In fiscal years 2005 and 2006, the service "reported that there was insufficient staff to conduct adequate analysis of civilian workforce data," and in 2004, 2005, and 2006, the service noted it "has not implemented an adequate data collection and analysis system and had not tracked recruitment efforts." The EEOC found that the Coast Guard's recruitment practices for positions in the civilian workforce created "unintended barriers" to diversity.

Having read all this, what was perhaps most disappointing to me was not just the devastating nature of these individual findings, but the fact that the problems they describe have apparently persisted for nearly a decade. Put simply, the picture that emerges from the reports available to us shows that despite knowing that its equal opportunity programs did not ensure full compliance with U.S. law and regulations, the Coast Guard has taken little to no action to ensure full compliance. Further, there have apparently been no consequences for these failures – except perhaps the individual consequences that Coast Guard personnel may have borne, some of whom may have been denied the opportunity to effectively challenge what they may have felt was discriminatory treatment.

Discrimination is an evil that destroys the dignity of fellow human beings and robs them of the opportunity to achieve what their abilities would otherwise enable them to achieve. In this, the 21st Century, any agency that tolerates any failure in the implementation of effective equal employment opportunity processes or in the effective management of complaints is an agency that is willing to tolerate the possibility that discrimination may exist in its midst.

While I applaud the decision of the Director of the Office of Civil Rights to ask for an independent assessment of Coast Guard civil rights practices, it is also obvious that further study is not needed. Back in 2001, the KPMG team that assessed the Coast Guard's civil rights program reported that the wide gaps between how the service's equal employment opportunity program was described in manuals and how the program was actually implemented "created a perception that the program is not necessarily a priority among senior leadership." It is LONG PAST TIME that these gaps be closed.

Importantly, as the Booz|Allen|Hamilton report makes clear, successful implementation of the reforms needed to correct the gaps that their team found "will need to be openly endorsed at the highest level of the Coast Guard organization to ensure the cooperation of, and participation by, key stakeholders." I know that the Coast Guard is undertaking a variety of initiatives to expand diversity, and I commend the written testimony of Admiral Breckenridge, which details these efforts. I also commend the individual efforts of Coast Guard personnel to support the service's diversity goals. I note that Admiral Allen himself recently visited Morgan State University in my district and gave a very inspiring address to students at that Historically Black University. What I didn't find in Admiral Breckenridge's testimony, however, was a statement that the MD-715 process will now be used as intended to identify all barriers to equal access and to inform the development of the plans that will eliminate these barriers, or that a similar process will be implemented on the military slide. While I appreciate discussion of an "upward glide slope," progress cannot be measured until specific goals are in place – and to think that goals would need to be defined as "specific representational objectives" is simply to think too narrowly.

I also commend Director Dickerson's testimony, and her decision to request the Booz|Allen|Hamilton review. I emphasize that I understand – as the Booz|Allen|Hamilton report indicates and the evidence clearly shows – that many of the problems with the Coast Guard's civil rights program have long pre-dated her appointment.

That said, it is now our watch and the failures and deficiencies that exist with the Coast Guard's civil rights programs CANNOT CONTINUE. For the Coast Guard to truly be "Semper Paratus" – always ready – it must take all necessary steps to ensure that it is not handicapped by discrimination in its ranks or the divisions that discrimination produces

CHAPTER 19

IF A MAN FALLS SHALL HE RISE AGAIN?

We, as Americans, believe in fairness, second chances and new beginnings. We like story book endings and fairy tales where the people live happily ever after. Even in our dramas and tragedies the good guy gets the girl; wrong is defeated and right triumphs. Despite the circumstances Webster Smith remained positive.

Lindsey Deason was the consummate competitive female athlete. And she was Webster Smith's Dream Girl.

They were married in a tropical paradise.

Their first child was a daughter, <u>Alexis Leigh Smith</u>.

Webster, Lindsey and Alexis were able to rise from the ashes and create a new life for themselves. They left all of the accusations, recriminations and acrimony behind them. They walked into a new life.

CHAPTER 20

THE BOLD AND THE BEAUTIFUL. WHERE THIS STORY BEGINS

Everyone who has lived long enough to experience the complete panoply of human events, knows that the real facts for most of life's events are usually lurking just beneath the surface. This is also true for the Webster Smith Story.

This is a story of love and hate, passion and jealousy. It is ripe with the innocence of young love, and female fury. It pitted two Type A-Alpha Females against each other. And Webster Smith found out first hand that Hell has no fury like a woman scorned.

Webster and Kristen loved each other deeply. They had a secret. Kristen became pregnant and had an abortion. Webster nursed her back to health for six months. He ran errands for her. He cared for her hand and foot.

Over the Thanksgiving Holidays in 2005, Kristin took leave and left Webster at the Academy. Katie Colella invited him to have Thanksgiving Dinner with her and her family. They picked him up at the Academy. Webster divulged Kristen's secret. He told Katie Colella. It proved to be a fatal error. Kristen started a fire storm that consumed Webster, his career and his family. It destroyed his parents' marriage, and his mother's physical and mental health.

At the Trial a friend testified that she was watching a movie with Webster in 2005 when Kristen walked in and said "How could you do that to me? How could you steal him from me," the witness, Bazinet, recalled Kristen yelling and screaming. "It was scary", she said.

Webster thought that Howard Baker was his friend. Howard Baker had eyes for Kristen. He informed her that Webster had divulged their secret, and that he was dating Katie Colella. That led to a fiery confrontation between Kristen and Katie.

On 4 December 2005 an allegation of sexual misconduct from a cadet, was relayed to the Chase Hall Duty Officer. All indications are that Kristine made the report . The Commandant of Cadets, Captain Douglas Wisniewski started an investigation. He requested the assistance of the Coast Guard Investigative Services (CGIS).

The trial was just too much for Belinda, Webster's mother. She exhibited great dignity and restraint. She was the most gracious lady under pressure in the public spot light since Coretta Scott King, Myrlie Evers, and Jackie Kennedy all rolled into one. They mourned the death of their husbands. Belinda mourned the sacrifice of her son, and the death of his Coast Guard career.

The civilian employees at the Academy could not help but notice, her poise and dignity under such enormous pressure. They were mothers and sisters. Webster could have been their son or brother. They were so moved that they were compelled to act. They had to reach out to her in a practical way. They presented her with a note and a gift. The card read,

> "We are so proud of the way you have carried yourself here, with much dignity and poise. Please take this small token of respect and do something nice for yourself. "

Belinda Smith found some relief in writing a journal. She reduced her thoughts to writing. This is a sample:

QUOTE:

" If you could only feel what I have felt for these past 6 years, I have a strong relationship with JUSTICE that I am not able to shake. People say, "get over it, get a life!" I cannot! I closely watch Webster's life and all of my children's lives after this tragedy, and I am amazed by the spirit within them. I sometimes think, I use to be able to overcome obstacles, (I had so many). If this is possible, I gave my spirit, my soul and my mind to my children, and they are using it to go on in life. Today though, I felt that in many ways I failed......I became an empty shell at one point in my life, soon after the death of my brother. Looking back, those are the moments when I knew my children's firm foundation was in place. I see it now in Webster, Brittney and the twins. They have been through a lot and look at them, still achieving and motivated to make it. That's why I said I failed them, I lost that! God's grace is sufficient. "

"The two weeks of the court-martial was very difficult for me, because as I've said before; I knew in my heart that Webster was being setup and I was sure when the evidence was heard, he would be exonerated. Somewhere along the way, I begin to tell myself, these people are not going to allow my son to walk out of here an innocent man that he is, because this would bring the Coast Guard to their knees. There is a lot I could say about this but I will not. Would I let another one of my sons go to the academy, well, one of my twin sons was determined to go the CGA, actually Alex was in the prep program a NMMI, until Capt. B decided not to accept him because he had a 2.4 GPA but accepted other cadets at NMMI that had a even lower GPA to go to the academy. That same year Kristen Nicholson's younger brother was accepted. Kristen said in an email to my daughter and me, and she actually said, I am doing what I was told to do and went on to say as I understood, you do what those over you tell you to do, There were two female cadets that came to the court-martial in support of Webster, but were afraid to say so, They would always come up to me and give me a hug. One even alluded to the fact that Jesse Harms would go from the court-martial to the upstairs law office where the girls were to tell them what was said in court. One day, I waited at the end of the stairs and yes he came down the stairs just as they said. I was also told that Shannon and Shelly were spending time together during the court-martial, and we actually saw them together at Panera's Bread when we all went to eat. I bought this up to LT Kirkby, Webster's Navy lawyer, and he did nothing about it. During the Court-martial, Admiral Van Sice came up to Webster and me, and he spoke to Webster and said something to the fact that , everything will be alright it will take some time."

"This is LIPSTICK JUSTICE that we have witness. Lipstick covers the lips in order to make them beautiful and when it wears off, you will see all the imperfections that is always there. The girls in this trial wore that lipstick and I will not rest until I see their bare lips. You may not understand my analogies, but it make sense to me. I know for sure that as I read further the record of trial, that night that those girls met, LTJG Miller said that there were 7 girls and so did the first reporting in the news. Then at trial she said there were seven (7) girls and later changed it to five (5) because the judge said and lead her to change it to 5, You know why, the second meeting that they had, Katie had told them about Shelly and Sheri and Kristen went to get those two. I know they are hiding that lie. Katie was the only person that knew about Shelly and Stacy was the only one that knew about Katie, When Stacy met with Kristen in their private meeting, Stacy told Kristen about Katie and that's how Kristen found out. They then went to Katie and confronted her about Webster and all she could do after that was to join in because she was angry possibly that Webster had told Stacy. Katie knew she had to save her face so she wrote a statement to keep her and her father out of trouble to appease them, but she had enough integrity not go alone with the "witch hunt". The biggest secret isn't Shelly's. it's the fact that they are covering up why Shelly did not want to come forward and bring charges against Webster until she was confronted by her regimental commander and the legal team, especially after they threaten to charge her with disobeying a direct order and article 125. They either falsified the date of Shelly's statement which is Feb.16th or they had to use undue command influence to get her to testify,,,,either way; it was unethical.

Even then, if the statement was written on Feb 16 why did they not give this to the Defense upon their Discovery Request? No, the defense did not know about Shelly until March 8th when Anderson sent a letter stating, all witness has to on the list by March 10th. This caused the defense to have to delay the Article 32 to compose themselves. Sometimes, I think this was a plan to delay the trial so that they all could graduate before the trial began in order to convince Shelly she could get her degree, even if she was charged with any crime. At least she had her degree if they gave her walking papers.

"I know I will find a way to be heard! I am missing something! I pray for Katie and the other girls in this case and when I feel it's time, I will reach out. I have noticed that Katie no longer has friends from the Coast Guard on her Facebook. That may be because she has broken ties with them. I am researching and studying as much as I can from information from these sites. I have also noticed, that Kristen, Shelly, Kristen's friend "Jersey" who also testified are all pregnant or had babies before there 5 years were up. Kristen married Howard Baker the guy who told her about Katie's relationship with Webster.

UNQUOTE.

Most people know the basic premise of the story, the collusion of several young women that resulted in the court-martial of the first cadet at the U.S. Coast Guard Academy. Shelly Raudenbush Wyman was the lone victor of the several women that accounted for the 22 charges against Webster Smith. Why did she come forward over two months after Webster Smith was removed from classes, following the allegations by then Regimental Commander-Kristen Nicholson, her two best friends Shannon Frobel, Kristin Strizki and Nicholson's subordinates: Stacy Chmielecki, Keri McCormack, and Katie Colella?

During the Court-Martial, Webster was represented by LT Stuart Kirkby and Merle J. Smith. Neither believed that the charges would prevail for the government. They did not pursue details of Shelly's relationship with the other female cadets. They could not mention Katie

Colella or call her to the stand, Captain Judge, the Trial Judge at the court-martial, denied her as a defense witness. Besides Kristen Nicholson, she was the only person who could detail how and why she came forward. Her father had just been appointed the Dean of Students at the Academy and wanted no part of it. This was not the only reason that Smith's attorneys did not further pursue Shelly. Shelly Raudenbush Wyman was charged with two UCMJ violations--including disobeying an order--by the Coast Guard Academy, to push her to cooperate. She consulted with an attorney before the Smith trial and would not testify in the May pre-trial hearing so that she would not incriminate herself. The academy did not give her prosecutorial or testimonial immunity until the day she testified.

Why did she come forward?

The only cadet that knew about Webster and Shelly's sexual relationship was then-cadet Katie Colella.

Katie Colella and Webster went out several times in November of 2005. Over Thanksgiving Break when Webster decided to stay at the Academy, he picked her up from Captain Colella's home in Ledyard, Connecticut. They went out on the first of two or three dates, with the blessing of the Captain. The first night, they went to a club called Complex and outside of the Complex Webster told Katie about Shelly. Katie asked Webster to end it if he wanted to hang out with her.
Before the investigation, as the evidence revealed, Katie had not told the Regimental Commander about Shelly.

Katie played as integral of a role as Kristen Nicholson did in pushing the charges but when it came time to end Webster's career, she was nowhere on the charge sheet. The circumstances around their relationship could not be crafted for a charge sheet and maybe she had a little more integrity than the others.

In February of 2006 when CAPT Wisniewski realized that Webster was not going to plead guilty to the original charges, he stood before the Corps of Cadets in the Chase Hall wardroom and asked for any additional female cadets to testify against Webster Smith.

Katie Colella, Shelly's track teammate, told Kristen of the conversation about Shelly. Kristen, the acting Regimental Commander, approached Shelly (Shelly admitted in trial) and several days later, she was interviewed by CGIS

Not only was there a question of criminal prosecution for Shelly, she squelched rumors to save her engagement to Grant Wyman by agreeing to help the girls with Webster Smith. Shelly's fiance was not there to support her during any of the hearings or the trial. Shelly did not attend or testify against Webster at the sentencing hearing Katie Colella was later kicked out on an Honor Violation; but, she was readmitted later in the Spring of 2008. Several other senior officers' kids were readmitted after being kicked out. (Another cadet who was kicked out of the Coast Guard Academy because of an honor violation was the son of Admiral James Loy (retired). He was readmitted to the Academy in about1992, and then kicked out again for another Honor Violation. Then he goes through OCS and earns a commission despite his Academy background.)

Webster's continued relationship with Shelly was never allowed into evidence in court. Her lobbying Webster to join the track team, and her frequent trips to Webster's dorm room to comfort him after several issues that Webster had had with his ex-girlfriend, Kristen Nicholson, in early November were never allowed into evidence.

The Court of Appeals majority ruling stated that there was no reason for Shelly to misrepresent the truth in trial.

Even in civilian life, after a conviction and serving time in jail, Webster was not free from Coast Guard interference in his life. A web site was set up for his friends and family to keep in touch. It was shut down.

This entry was posted by cgreports.wordpress.com on June 11, 2009 at 6:26 pm and is filed under Uncategorized.

QUOTE: "We were notified today that Webster Smith, the first cadet to ever be courts-martialed at the U.S. Coast Guard Academy has had his site blocked by the U.S. Coast Guard. Smiths website "Friends of Webster" is not accessible inside the Coast Guard domain. We reviewed the site and couldn't find anything in our cursory review that would warrant being blocked."
UNQUOTE
(See-http://cgreport.wordpress.com/2009/06/11/webster-smith-former-u-s-coast-guard-academy-cadet-blocked-inside-coast-guard-domain/)

Were there any winners in the story? No. Everyone lost something. Kristen lost her faithful companion, their child, his family, and her reputation. She gained a husband, Howard B. Baker, Junior. He was Webster's best friend but he coveted Webster's girl. So, he set in motion the chain of events that lead to Kristen's accusations against Webster, and the Court-martial of Webster Smith.

The girls lost their innocence what little they had left after four years in a military officers' school.

Webster lost his career in the Coast Guard. He did not get his Bachelors of Science Degree or his Officer's Commission from the Academy. But , on May 17, 2008 Webster received his Bachelors of Arts and Sciences Degree in General Business and Decision and Information Science. Webster completed 41 credit hours in two semesters and graduated with Academic Distinction(for transfer students who will graduate with 36-59 UST hours, based on the grade point average at the end of the fall semester). Webster's tenacity, determination and perseverance was commendable. The excellent academic foundation he had received at Strake Jesuit College Prep, Naval Academy Prep, and Coast Guard Academy enabled him to successful achieve academic excellence at the University of St. Thomas (Houston's only Catholic University).

Webster Smith said it best.

QUOTE:

I graduated with honors with a degree in General Business and Decision Information Science from the University of St. Thomas. I completed a two semester Russian Linguistics program at Neighboring Rice University and completed all requirements for the pre-law designation. Emotional moment for my family, especially my father and me. On February 15th, 2006 the night before the Coast Guard Academy called me back to face allegations and a negative press barrage, we had a long talk. He took off his academy ring and I took mine off. He never had that ring off in my presence. He told me that he wouldn't put it back on until I walked across the stage. That motivated me more than any of the detractors could, so I finished my necessary 41 hours in 10 months. Seeing him cry, yesterday, broke me down. For a moment, we won.

UNQUOTE.

The Coast Guard lost. It lost the presumption of innocence and good faith when disciplining teenage cadets from diverse backgrounds. It lost its virginity with respect to military justice. When a fly swat would have served quite nicely, the Coast Guard pulled out a Howitzer.

Lindsey won. Her patience and her faith in Webster paid off. She gained a husband and a family. In that sense, Webster also won. Jump for joy. She gets to live happily ever after.

(Cleon Smith, above left, and Judge L. Steverson,
USALJ(Ret.) circa May 2016)

NOTES

1. Rainey, Richard; AP article, January 21, 2006. Coast Guard Academy Investigating Male Cadet for Sexual Misconduct.
2. Rainey, Richard; AP article, February 17, 2006. Coast Guard Cadet Charged With Rape.
3. Rainey, Richard; AP article, February 25, 2006. Cadet Kicked Out Instead of Prosecuted.
4. Rainey, Richard; AP article, March 21, 2006. Coast Guard Cadet's Rape Hearing Begins.
5. Kime, Patricia, Navy Times, Mar. 27, 2006. *Academy Takes Heat Over Sex-Assault Cases*.
6. Rainey, Richard; AP article, April 13, 2006. Coast Guard Cadet to be Court-Martialed.
7. Rainey, Richard; AP article, June 20, 2006. Coast Guard Cadet's Accuser Testifies.
8. Rainey, Richard; AP article, June 22, 2006. New Witness Testifies in Cadet Rape Trial.
9. Rainey, Richard; AP article, June 26, 2006. Women Describe A Life Of Drinking, Partying And Sexual Favors. Trial Shows Another Coast Guard Academy.
10. Rainey, Richard; AP article, June 26, 2006. The Accused Cadet Takes The Witness Stand.
11. Rainey, Richard; AP article, June 27, 2006. Deliberations Start in Cadet's Rape Trial.
12. Apuzzo, Matt; AP article, July 3, 2006. After The Trial, A Time To Rethink Sexual Harassment Training.
13. New York Times editorial, July 1, 2006. Scandal At The Coast Guard Academy.

14. Manning, Stephen; AP article, July 7, 2006. Academies See Spike In Sexual Offenses.

15. Apuzzo, Matt; AP article, July 12, 2006. Coast Guard Academy Vows to Fight Attacks.

16. Apuzzo, Matt; AP article, February 22, 2006. Coast Guard Academy to Require Females on Sex Assault Cases.

17. CBS/AP News Article, New Haven, CT. December 18, 2006, Congressman Christopher Shays Calls For Investigation Of Sexual Assaults In The Military. CONGRESS TO INVESTIGATE SEX ASSAULTS IN MILITARY.

18. Smith, M. J., The Day, February 20, 2008, The Bottom Line On The Webster Smith Court-martial.

19. Howard, Lee, The Day, Dec. 28, 2010, Supreme Court Won't Hear Appeal In Conviction Of Former CGA Cadet.

20. Ogletree Jr., Charles J; The Presumption of Guilt: The Arrest of Henry Louis Gates Jr. and Race, Class, and Crime in America, Palgrave and Macmillan.

21. Grogan, Jennifer, The Day, CGA official: Inappropriate Sexual Behavior Has No Place at Coast Guard Academy, Jan. 9,2009.

22. Cose, Ellis. "Color-Blind (Seeing Beyond Race In A Race-Obsessed World)", (HarperCollins NY, NY, 1st Ed, 1997).

23. Friedman, Lawrence M.. "A History of American Law", (Touchstone, Simon & Schuster, Inc., New York, NY, 3rd Ed, 2005).

24. Wise, Tim. "White Like Me (Reflections on Race from a Privileged Son)", (Soft Skull Press, Brooklyn, NY, 2005).

25. Grogan, Jennifer, Two Cadets Appeal Dismissal From CGA, The Day Staff Writer, Defense & EB, Jan 17, 2007.

26. Grogan, Jennifer, Former cadets May Have Charges Dropped, The Day Staff Writer, Defense & EB, Oct. 10, 2007.

27. .United States v. Rogers, FB note, 2 June 2016, by Bill Cassara, Military Defense Attorney.

28. . U. S. v. Matthew A. Rogers, Unpublished Decision of USCAAF No. 16-0006/CG, Crim. App. No. 1391, Argued 15 March 2016, Decided 16 May 2016.

APPENDIXES

Appendix 1

A Letter To The Convening Authority

RADM James C. Van Sice
Superintendent, U. S. Coast Guard Academy
31 Mohegan Avenue
New London, CT. 06320-81003

RE: U. S. v Webster Smith

Dear RADM Van Sice:

I believe a terrible miscarriage of justice occurred upon the conviction of Web Smith, the first in the history of the Coast Guard. While it's apparent a conviction occurred, what's not apparent is the silence that has occurred among the prosecution and yourself in response to this terrible turn of events.

Having a father in the Merchant Marine for the last Sixty years, my admiration of the Coast Guard has been nothing but respect up until this point.

Please rest assured that more publicity will occur as the public sees exactly what transpired. Please understand that I am upset that you and your staff would be so quick to convict an innocent man. The jury had its hands tied due to the rules that were placed upon them.

While I am not a lawyer, as a Black Disease Intervention Specialist working for a local government, I have seen criminals up close and personal. I know how they think. Mr. Webb is not a criminal. What happened here was jealously, and vengeance by a bunch of old Coast Guard "good old boys" for Mr. Smith dating a bunch of white females.

The entire process from the selection of prosecution to the jury selection was flawed. The only evidence was the word of a couple of incredible females. No physical evidence whatsoever. In essence, a white word against a black word. We know how history reflects the word of a black man, much less in a court martial case with no physical evidence.

The failure of having the females testify before the defense amounts to a military lynching. Not only was Mr. Smith lynched once by having these ridiculous accusations brought against him, but twice by not having the females testify under oath.

Mr. Sice, it takes two to tango. Sodomy, more specifically oral sex has to be a willing give and receive. In my clinic, we see patients receive many sexually transmitted diseases as a consequence of unprotected oral sex. Once again, it takes two to tango. Both are willing participants. It doesn't seem reasonable that Mr. Smith gave oral sex to an unwilling female cadet unless she verbally said no, or physically denied Mr. Smith from going down on her. It appeared that this did not happen.

So, why proceed to convict Mr. Smith without convicting the rest of the female cadets? What's good for goose is not good for the gander? Mr. Sice, please reverse the conviction of this young man, and restore the integrity of the Coast Guard. Go after the real rapists in the academy, not after a bunch of horny cadets.

Best,

███████

Disease Intervention Specialist
SKC Public Health

Appendix 2

A Letter To The Southern Poverty Law Center

July 18, 2006
Mr. Morris Dees
Southern Poverty Law Center
400 Washington Avenue
P.O. Box 5632
Montgomery, AL. 36177-7459

RE: Cadet WEBSTER SMITH-U.S. Coast Guard Academy
Dear Morris,
As a member of the Leadership Council of the Law Center I am writing to ask you to get involved in the Cadet Webster Smith case. The legal team at the Law Center represents those who have no other champion. I have seen the good results that the Center has achieved over the years. I know that you share my passion for truth, justice, and equal justice under the law.

A case of gross injustice and rampant racial discrimination has occurred at the Coast Guard Academy. A graduating senior has been falsely accused, convicted on perjured testimony, and sentenced to six months in jail, expulsion from the Academy, and forfeiture of all pay and allowances. His name is Webster Smith and he is Black. He had been separated from the cadet student body six months before the court-martial and was forced to work on the boat docks. This amounted to essentially a sentence of hard labor before a trial. Moreover, since he is from Houston, Texas, he will have to register as a sex offender. That mark will follow him for the rest of his life, unless we can reverse the conviction.

The Associated Press characterized the trial as follows: "What began as a trial against an accused sexual predator ended looking more like a series of murky encounters between college students, with consent often clouded by alcohol. But the case also offered a rare and often unflattering glimpse at cadet life." (Moment of change' following Coast Guard Academy court-martial By MATT APUZZO Associated Press Writer, July 3, 2006.)

The Superintendent of the Coast Guard Academy has been asked to release Cadet Webster Smith from prison, reinstate him as a cadet, let him finish school, and graduate him with a commission. Our pleas have fallen on deaf ears.

Cadet Webster Smith is a victim of jealousy, racial discrimination, a violation of the 14th Amendment Equal Protection clause, and last but not the least, a victim of a double standard.

He was one of the most loved and respected cadets on campus. But he had two things going against him. One, he had dated the Regimental Commander, and the Dean of Admissions' daughter. Both were white. Since they were white and Cadet Smith was Black, it did not sit well with the Commandant of Cadets. Racial Prejudice is still very much alive at the Academy.

Moreover, when a REAL RAPE case with REAL physical evidence surfaced during Webster Smith's ordeal, Commandant of Cadets, Doug Wisniewski and his staff hushed the case, asked the white cadet to resign quietly and go on his way. NO CHARGES were filed. The real rapist was WHITE!

More facts and background on this case can be found at my web Blog spot at www.cgachasehall.blogspot.com.

I urgently beg you to direct the excellent resources of the Law Center to this case. Just a request for an explanation from the Superintendent of the Coast Guard Academy would be a tremendous help. Just to get involved with this case will send a loud and clear message that will prevent similar abuses in the future. This case could do a lot to bring positive advertisement and increase respect for the Law Center worldwide. Webster Smith's picture has gone around the word. This case presents you with a fundraising bonanza.

Yours Respectfully,
L. Steverson,
LCDR, USCG (Ret.)

Appendix 3

A Letter To The NAACP

July 17, 2006
Mr. Julian Bond
Chairman, NAACP
National Board of Directors
4805 Hope Drive
Baltimore, MD. 21215-3297

RE: Cadet WEBSTER SMITH- U.S. Coast Guard Academy
Dear Mr. Bond:
This is in furtherance of my letter to you of July 10, 2006 concerning
Cadet Webster Smith. He continues to be held in jail. After his court-
martial, Cadet Web Smith was taken to the U.S. Navy brig at the
Submarine Base in Groton, Connecticut on 28 June 2006. Originally he
was supposed to be transferred on 10 July to a Federal prison for
military officers in South Carolina. It did not happen, nor has the
Admiral signed off on the Report of the Court-martial. The delay has not
been explained. The new plans are to transfer him to the South Carolina
prison on 19 July. That day might not be accurate either, unless the
Admiral intends to deliberately violate Commandant Instruction
M5350.4B, The Civil Rights Manual, which requires the Academy Civil
Rights Officer to attempt to resolve informally a civil rights complaint
within 5 days of receiving it. Joann Miller, the Academy Civil Rights
Officer, plans to retire on 28 July. If she lets Webster Smith get out of
town before she can attempt an informal resolution, then she will have to
spend the remainder of her tour of duty commuting between New
London and South Carolina. A copy of the Civil Rights Complaint is
attached.

Cadet Webster has not seen or talked to his mother or father since June 28, 2006. They have his power of attorney. They signed the original Complaint.

This is a case of gross injustice and rampant racial discrimination at the Coast Guard Academy. A graduating senior has been falsely accused, convicted on perjured testimony, and sentenced to six months in jail, expulsion from the Academy, and forfeiture of all pay and allowances. His name is Webster Smith and he is Black. He had been separated from the cadet student body six months before the court-martial and was forced to work on the boat docks. This amounted to essentially to a sentence of hard labor before a trial. Moreover, since he is from Houston, Texas, he will have to register as a sex offender. That mark will follow him for the rest of his life, unless we can reverse the conviction.

The Superintendent of the Coast Guard Academy has been asked to release Cadet Webster Smith from prison, reinstate him as a cadet, let him finish school, and graduate him with a commission. Our pleas have fallen on deaf ears.

Cadet Webster Smith is a victim of jealousy, racial discrimination, a violation of the 14th Amendment Equal Protection clause, and last but not the least, a victim of a double standard.

He was one of the most loved and respected cadets on campus. But he had two things going against him. One, he had dated the Regimental Commander, and the Dean of Admissions' daughter. Both were white. Since they were white and Cadet Smith was Black, it did not sit well with the Commandant of Cadets. Racial Prejudice is still very much alive at the Academy.

Moreover, when a REAL RAPE case with REAL physical evidence surfaced during Webster Smith's ordeal, Commandant of Cadets, Doug Wisniewski and his staff hushed the case, asked the white cadet to resign quietly and go on his way. NO CHARGES were filed. The real rapist was WHITE?

More facts and background on this case can be found at my web Blog spot at www.cgachasehall.blogspot.com.

Yours Respectfully,
Judge L. Steverson,
Silver Life Member NAACP

Appendix 4

Letter From Admiral James Van Sice to USCGA Alumni

Subject: Webster Smith Update

Classmates,

Attached is a note from the new Assistant Superintendent of the Academy, Captain Dan May, '79. All the class correspondents were asked to forward this note to their classmates. I forward it to you without comment.

Many of you have also asked for specific contact info for RADM Van Sice. In the interest of fairness, I have included it as well.

Rear Admiral James C. Van Sice US Coast Guard Academy 31 Mohegan Ave New London, Ct 6320- 8103

James.c.VanSice@uscg.mil

Regards,
XXXXX

Attached is his letter.................

To all CGA Alumni and the Coast Guard Community:

This past January, CAPT Jim Thomas, who then served in my current position as the Assistant Superintendent of the Academy, informed you of a sexual misconduct investigation involving a member of the CGA Corps of Cadets. For those that have continued to follow along the past 6 months, you are well aware that the investigation led to formal charges against a First Class cadet and ultimately a court-martial, the first for an Academy cadet in the history of CGA. I want to take this opportunity to once again reach out to you with some updated information as we continue to move forward and make progress.

Our system of military justice is designed to ensure that all cases are resolved in a just manner. We endeavor to ensure a thorough and professional investigation of allegations brought to the command's attention. The unique facts and circumstances of each case are assessed to determine its appropriate disposition. When a general court-martial is contemplated, an impartial Investigating Officer is selected to assess the evidence and offer recommendations. Accused service members are detailed defense counsel and allowed individual military counsel and/or civilian defense counsel of their choosing. Cases are heard by impartial, qualified court members, before trained Military Judges, in open and transparent proceedings. Fact finders are charged to decide cases weighing the evidence against the high burden of proof imposed on the government. Our commitment to justice, due process and the rule of law requires faithful observance of the processes established by the Rules for Courts-Martial.

Several weeks ago, the CGA court-martial concluded with the First Class Cadet acquitted of five charges (rape, extortion, sodomy, assault and unlawful entry) and convicted of five other charges (extortion, sodomy, indecent assault, attempted failure to obey a lawful order and unauthorized absence). The court-martial members adjudged 6 months confinement, forfeiture of all pay/allowances and dismissal from the service. Although the trial has concluded, the case continues in the post-trial processing phase, which includes the convening authority's (CGA Superintendent) action. After reviewing the results of trial, clemency materials submitted by the defense, and the Staff Judge Advocate's recommendation, the convening authority may disapprove a finding of guilty, and/or approve, disapprove, mitigate or change a punishment (as long as the severity of the punishment is not increased).

The post-trial processing phase can take several months to conclude. While this process unfolds, it is critically important that the convening authority absent himself from engaging in any direct comments concerning the case or the specific outcome.

A case of this nature evokes strong opinion and sentiments among all involved as well as the casual observer. This case has been no exception. Many of you have expressed your views in various venues including emails and letters to CGA. However, until the case is officially resolved, it would be inappropriate for CGA or the convening authority to discuss the particulars of this case in any forum outside
the court-martial process.

Thus, I ask for your continued understanding and patience as this case makes its way towards a final conclusion. Just as Jim did, I also want to reiterate that the Coast Guard Academy is founded on the Coast Guard's core values of Honor, Respect and Devotion to duty. We will never waiver from our commitment to these precious values. We are also committed to the fair treatment of all members of our service.

Just two weeks ago, 274 new cadets reported to CGA, marched onto Washington Parade field and took the oath of service as the Class of 2010. They are some of the best young people our nation has to offer and they are extremely committed to the Coast Guard. They are honored and proud to be at this institution. They are the future of our service. We owe it to them to remain strong and to never waiver from
our service commitments.

v/r, D. R. May, CAPT, USCG Assistant Superintendent U.S. Coast Guard Academy

Appendix 5

First Word Of Protest Against This Appalling Injustice.

By Richard Rainey (AP)

New London — A former officer who led early racial integration efforts at the U.S. Coast Guard Academy has called the June 28 conviction of a black cadet on sodomy and extortion charges an example of "rampant" racial discrimination at the school.

London Steverson, a 1968 graduate of the academy, wrote NAACP chairman Julian Bond July 10 demanding a full investigation into whether the cadet's civil rights had been violated. His letter is at the leading edge of a growing intervention effort for the former academy student.

"Cadet Webster Smith is a victim of jealousy, racial discrimination, a violation of the 14th Amendment Equal Protection clause, and last but not least, a victim of a double standard," Steverson wrote.

Smith, 23, of Houston, was acquitted last month of a charge of rape but convicted on five lesser charges, including those related to extorting a female classmate to provide him with sexual favors.

The eight-day general court-martial, which took place last month in the academy's Hamilton Hall, was the first top-level trial of a cadet in the school's 130-year history.

Smith is now serving a six-month prison sentence after being convicted of extortion, sodomy, indecent assault, leaving his post without permission and attempting to disobey an order. The female cadets and officers who testified against him were white.

"Racial prejudice is still very much alive at the academy," Steverson wrote.

Steverson, who is Black and a member of the NAACP, now serves as a federal judge in California. From 1972 to 1974, he was assigned to lead the Coast Guard's newly formed minority recruiting section. During his tenure, he recruited more than 50 Black cadets to the academy. Before that only four Black officers, including Steverson, had graduated from the school. He retired from the Coast Guard as a lieutenant in 1987.

It remained unclear Thursday whether the NAACP would be looking into the matter. The organization is amid preparations for its annual convention this month. Bond could not be reached for comment in several attempts this week.

Several people have said they have written to the academy superintendent, Rear Adm. James C. Van Sice, in support of Smith. As the highest-ranking officer at the academy, Van Sice has the authority to uphold, reduce or even eliminate Smith's sentence.

Eddie A. Richards, a friend and academy classmate of Smith's father, Cleon Smith, said a coalition of supporters has formed to petition Van Sice to free the former cadet.

"All I can say is Cleon, myself and other Coast Guard alumni of that school are ripped apart because of our love for the school," he said in a telephone interview. "We felt we have tried to let the system work."

Richards said he was in contact with an attorney looking into the case.

Steverson wrote Van Sice June 29, a day after Smith's conviction, demanding the verdict be overturned. Steverson said he has not received a response.

"I was hoping cooler heads could prevail, and we could resolve this issue at this level," Steverson said in a telephone interview Wednesday. "I can only presume that (Van Sice) is stonewalling."

An academy spokesman, Chief Warrant Officer David M. French, said the superintendent's office is preparing a response to Steverson's letter. French declined further comment.

The academy began admitting Black students in 1962. Merle J. Smith Jr. of Quaker Hill, who acted as Webster Smith's civilian defense counsel, was the school's first Black graduate in 1966.

Click name for author info, most recent articles ...
Published on 7/14/2006 in Region » Region News
r.rainey@theday.com

Appendix 6

This Is The Ultimate Issue On Appeal As Decided By The Trial Judge, Captain Brian Judge

GENERAL COURT-MARTIAL
UNITED STATES COAST GUARD
UNITED STATES
v.
WEBSTER M. SMITH, CADET, U.S. COAST GUARD
FILED UNDER SEAL[*]

MEMORANDUM ORDER AND OPINION
M.R.E. 413 [sic] EVIDENCE CADET [SR]

The Defense has provided notice that it intends to introduce evidence of specific instances of sexual behavior involving then Cadet, now Ensign [SR]. This alleged sexual behavior is the subject of the secret that Cadet Smith is charged with threatening to expose in Specification I of Additional Charge II. The Government seeks to bar the introduction of such evidence pursuant to M.R.E. 412. At the Article 39(a) session held on 23 May 2006, Ensign [SR] did not testify because she invoked her right under Article 31(b) to consult with an attorney. The accused testified as to the content of his conversations with Cadet [SR] on this subject. The Defense also submitted a written statement dated 15 February 2006 that Cadet [SR] provided to the Coast Guard Investigative Service.

FINDINGS OF FACT

During the summer training program at the start
of their first class year, Cadet Smith and Cadet [SR] were both assigned to patrol boats that moored at Station Little Creek. Both lived in

210

barracks rooms at the Station. In May 2005, Cadet Smith approached Cadet [SR] to inform her that he was hearing rumors from the enlisted personnel assigned to the Station that she had
a sexual encounter with an enlisted member assigned to the Station. Cadet [SR] told him that this was true, but that it was not a consensual encounter. Cadet Smith then informed the enlisted personnel who were spreading the rumors that the conduct was not consensual.

On or about 19 October 2005, Cadet Smith again approached Cadet [SR]. He told her that he had remained in contact with some of the enlisted personnel assigned to Station Little Creek and that the rumors surrounding her sexual encounter with the enlisted man had continued. This time she told him that the incident with the enlisted man had been a consensual encounter and that scope of the encounter had been greater than she had previously described.

At the Article 32 hearing, Cadet [SR] merely stated that she had confided a secret to Cadet Smith.

In her 15 February 2006 statement, she merely stated that a situation occurred which led to rumors. On both occasions, she went on to state that on October 19th, she was concerned enough that Cadet Smith would expose this secret that **she agreed to pose for a picture with him in which both of them were nude, and later that night allowed him to perform cunnilingus on her then she performed fellatio on him.**

CONCLUSIONS OF LAW

Generally, evidence that an alleged victim of a sexual offense engaged in other sexual behavior or evidence of the alleged victim's sexual predisposition is not admissible. M.R.E. 412(a). There are three exceptions to this general rule, but only one may be relevant here: evidence of the sexual behavior of the victim is admissible if excluding the evidence would violate the constitutional rights of the accused. M.R.E. 412(b)(1)(C). This exception protects the accused's Sixth Amendment right to confront witnesses and Fifth Amendment right to a fair trial. *United States v. Banker*, 60 M.J. 216, 221 (2004). In other words, the accused has a right to produce relevant evidence that is material and favorable to his defense. *Id.* Evidence is relevant if it tends to make the existence of any fact more or less probable than it would be without the evidence. M.R.E. 401. Assuming these requirements are met, the accused must also demonstrate that the probative value of the evidence outweighs the danger of unfair prejudice. M.R.E. 412(c)(3). In this context, the unfair prejudice is, in part, to the privacy interests of the alleged victim. *Banker*, 60 M.J. at 223. M.R.E. 412 is a legislative recognition of the high value we as a society place on keeping our sexual behavior private.

The Defense offered several theories of why this evidence is admissible. First, the Defense wanted to introduce this evidence to impeach the credibility of Ensign [SR] when she testifies. The general rule is that a witness' credibility may be attacked in the form of an opinion or by reputation concerning the witness' character for truthfulness. M.R.E. 608(a). Specific instances of conduct of witness may be admitted, at the discretion of the military judge, if probative of truthfulness. I decline to exercise that discretion in this case because I believe that, under these circumstances, the probative value of this evidence is substantially outweighed by the danger of unfair prejudice. Then Cadet [SR] was under no duty to be completely forthcoming with Cadet Smith concerning her private life, particularly under these circumstances since her rumored conduct would be in violation of Coast Guard regulations and could subject her to disciplinary action or other adverse consequences. More important, despite any limiting instruction, members might consider this evidence less for its tendency to prove Ensign [SR]'s character for truthfulness than for its tendency to prove that she is a bad person. Finally, conflicting testimony on this point from

Ensign [SR] and Cadet Smith could easily sidetrack members from testimony regarding the charged offenses which the member's should be focusing on.

The Defense also argued that the members must know the substance of Cadet [SR]'s secret in order for them to independently assess whether or not she would feel coerced into taking a nude photograph with Cadet Smith and later engaging in mutual oral sex in order to protect that secret. While the importance of her secret would be relevant in this fashion, I do not think that the members would need to know the specifics. At the Article 39(a) session, the Government offered a generic formulation that would impress upon the members the seriousness of the secret. In essence, the members could be informed that the secret was information that if revealed could have an adverse impact on her Coast Guard career, including possibly disciplinary action under the UCMJ.

The final rationale offered by the Defense at the Article 39(a) hearing is the most persuasive. The Defense argued that if the members hear that Cadet [SR] originally told Cadet Smith that a sexual encounter with another man was non-consensual, and then later admitted that it in fact was consensual, then the members could use this testimony to infer that the same thing is happening in this case. In other words, the members could infer that Cadet [SR] has a propensity to bring false accusations against men with whom she has had consensual sexual encounters. I agree that this theory would be a valid reason for admitting this evidence under M.R.E. 412(b)(1)(C), but there are two problems with the Defense proffer. First, the evidence proffered that Cadet [SR] made these statements is not strong since it comes from the accuse d, who has an obvious bias. Cadet [SR]'s written statement and Article 32 testimony on this point is not clear. She admitted at the Article 32 that she only partially confided in Cadet Smith in May and fully confided in him on October 19th; however, this is far from proof that she initially claimed that the encounter was non-consensual. In fact, it is consistent with the rest of Cadet Smith's Article 39(a) testimony that on October 19th she told him that the scope of the sexual encounter had been greater than she had previously described. The probative value of this evidence is therefore low.

More important, there is no evidence that Cadet [SR] made an official complaint against the unnamed enlisted man. Even if Cadet [SR] told the accused in May that the encounter was not consensual, the nature of this confidential statement is far different from the nature of her statements to law enforcement personnel that she must have known would result in a public prosecution. Cadet [SR]'s alleged statement to Cadet Smith was apparently intended to keep more people from learning about her sexual encounter with the enlisted man. It was not a false complaint to law enforcement. In contrast, her statements made in this case were to law enforcement personal and would certainly lead to a public prosecution. Consequently, even if Cadet [SR] falsely told the accused *in confidence* that her sexual encounter with the enlisted man was nonconsensual *in an effort to suppress rumors*, this would have little value in proving that her *official* allegations against Cadet Smith *resulting in **a public trial*** are also false. I am convinced that the minimal probative value of this evidence is outweighed by danger of unfair prejudice to Ensign [SR]'s privacy interests and the potential danger of sidetracking the member's attention to a collateral issue as described in paragraph 2 above.

For the above reasons, the Government's objection that this evidence is inadmissible in accordance with M.R.E. 413 [sic] is **SUSTAINED**.

EFFECTIVE DATE
This order was effective on 26 May 2006.
Done at Washington, DC,
/s/
Brian Judge
Captain, U.S. Coast Guard
Military Judge

APPENDIX 7

Dissenting Opinion of **The Coast Guard Court of Criminal Appeals**

The U.S. Coast Guard Court of Criminal Appeals had to review the Webster Smith case. It had no choice. Article 66 of the Uniform Code of Military Justice, requires the Coast Guard Criminal appeals Court to review all cases of trial by court-martial in which the sentence as approved by the Convening Authority extends to dismissal of a cadet from the Coast Guard, and/or a dishonorable or bad conduct discharge, unless the accused waives appellate review. Webster Smith did not waive appellate review. He appealed his conviction. Oral arguments in the Case of The Appeal of the Court-martial Conviction of Cadet Webster Smith was scheduled for January 16, 2008 in Arlington, Virginia.

A legal brief filed by his lawyers claimed the convictions should have been thrown out because the defense team was not allowed to fully cross-examine one of his accusers during Smith's court martial. They said that meant the jury didn't hear testimony that the accuser, a female cadet, Shelly Roddenbush, had once had consensual sex with a Coast Guard enlisted man and then called it sexual assault. If she lied once, she very well could have lied again.

The Coast Guard Court of Criminal Appeals is made up of Coast Guard Officers. It has the power to decide matter of both fact and law. Decisions of the Coast Guard Court of Criminal Appeals may be appealed to the Court of Appeals of the Armed Forces (CAAF). It is made up of five civilian judges, appointed to 15 year terms. It decides only issues of law. Its decisions may be appealed to the U. S. Supreme

Court. The Webster Smith Case followed this long and winding path all the way to the Supreme Court.

The Coast Guard Court of Criminal Appeals by a narrow margin made the wrong decision for the wrong reason. They have left the Sixth Amendment to the U S Constitution in shreds. {Footnote.(1)} By **a majority of 2-1**, they voted against Webster Smith.

The Decision was not unanimous. It was a majority opinion. Only one member of the Appellate Court was able to see clearly the errors made by the Trial Court and to vote his conscious.

I see no reason to waste m time reciting the strained, biased, and contorted illogic of the Majority Opinion. Chief Judge Lane I McClleland was determined to affirm the conviction, no matter how rediculous the decision read. It will forever stand as one more piece of evidence to history and to the majority of reasonable people as to just how institutionally biased the Coast Guard Military Justice apparatus really is.

The dissenting opinion was more persuasive. In a clear, cogent and convincing analysis that flowed logically, **the dissent** appears to has fashioned a minority opinion that **could easily become the majority opinion** if the Supreme Court grants Certiorari. It was a masterpiece of scholarly legal reasoning that is sure to take its place with the likes of Learned Hand, Oliver Wendell Holmes, and Thurgood Marshall.

The 2 judge Majority opinion assumed such a contorted illogical path that it resembled a pretzel draped out in a straight-jacket; whereas, the Minority opinion is so straight and logical, it could show the way to San Jose. It should be christened "stare decisis".

The Coast Guard Court of Criminal Appeals when Webster Smith was decided was constituted as follows:

Acting Chief Judge Lane I. McClelland

Judge David J. Kantor
Judge Thomas R. Cahill
Judge Gary E. Felicetti
Judge Frederick W. **Tucher**
Judge Michael J. Lodge
Clerk of the Court: Jane R. Lim

Judge Frederick W. **Tucher, t**he judge who wrote the Minority opinion should be commended. He not only has courage but also a brilliant legal mind. His only fault is that he could not convince at least one of the other two judges on the three judge panel to see the error of their ways.

The Dissent:

TUCHER, Judge (concurring in part and dissenting in part):

I concur with the majority decision on Assignments **II,** IV, V, and VI.__ I dissent from the decision on Assignments **I** and **III.**

I agree with the majority opinion that admission of the underlying details of SR's secret—namely, her prior sexual encounter with an enlisted member was subject to some limitation under Military Rule of Evidence (M.R.E.) 412. **I** would find, however, that the military judge abused his discretion when he prohibited the defense from cross-examining SR on her false statement to Appellant that the encounter was nonconsensual, since this evidence was highly probative of the defense theory that SR engaged in a pattern of fabrication to avoid discipline. As discussed below, **I** believe that the military judge erred when he decided the admissibility of this evidence **based on his own credibility determination** of the only two witnesses involved. The military judge also erred in not considering important factors that favored admission of the defense evidence, including that the Government made **first** use of evidence of SR's secret in its case-in-chief to prove that she was extorted and coerced into sexual relations with Appellant; that SR's credibility was a key element in an otherwise

218

uncorroborated case; and that the strength of the Government's case turned on the members finding the presence of subtle psychological influences that overcame SR's will. The excessive restrictions imposed on Appellant's Sixth Amendment confrontation rights allowed SR to testify through non-factual euphemisms on critical issues related to the Government's proof and her own credibility, and allowed the Government to create a substantially different impression of her truthfulness than what the defense had sought to show through the excluded evidence.

It is well-settled that "a primary interest secured by [the confrontation clause of the Sixth Amendment] is the right of cross-examination." *Douglas v. Alabama*, 380 U.S. 415, 418 (1965). "Cross-examination is the principal means by which the believability of a witness and the truth of his testimony are tested." *Davis v. Alaska*, 415 U.S. 308, 316 (1974). Moreover, "the exposure of a witness' motivation in testifying is a proper and important function of the constitutionally protected right of cross-examination." *Id.* at 316-17. In military courts-martial, the right to attack the partiality of a witness is primarily secured under M.R.E. 608(c), which provides for the admission of evidence that shows bias, prejudice, or any motive to misrepresent through cross-examination of witnesses or extrinsic evidence. *See United States v. Hunter*, 21 M.J. 240, 242

(C.M.A. 1986); *United States v. Saferite*, 59 M.J. 270 (C.A.A.F. 2004).

Although trial judges have broad discretion to impose reasonable limits on cross-examination to address concerns over harassment, prejudice, confusion of the issues, the witness' safety, or interrogation that is repetitive or only marginally relevant, this discretion is not without boundaries. Where the accuracy and truthfulness of the witness' testimony are "key elements" in the Government's case, a **trial** court's refusal to allow the defendant to cross-examine the witness regarding possible bias, motive, or prejudice is a violation of his **Sixth** Amendment rights. *Davis*, 415 U.S. at 317-18; *see also Saferite*, 59 M.J. at 273 ("Evidence of bias can be powerful impeachment."); *United States v. Moss*, 63 M.J. 233, 236 (C.A.A.F. 2006) ("When the military judge excludes evidence of bias, the exclusion raises issues regarding an accused's Sixth Amendment right to confrontation."); *United States v. Bins*, 43 M.J. 79, 84 (C.A.A.F. 1995) ("When the defense offers this evi- dence, it may deny confrontation rights to exclude it.");
United States v. Foster, 986 F.2d 541, 543 (D.C. Cir. 1993) ("The more important the witness to the government's case, the more important the defendant's right, derived from the Confrontation Clause of the Sixth Amendment, to cross-examine the witness.").

Evidence that SR had made a prior false claim of sexual assault to Appellant should have been admissible at trial because the central issue was whether SR consented during their sexual encounter on 19 October 2005, and SR was the only Government witness on the issue of consent. The defense should have been able to show that because SR had falsely informed Appellant that her prohibited sexual encounter with an enlisted member was nonconsensual, members could infer that

she had followed a similar scheme in fabricating a false complaint of indecent assault against Appellant, where the motive underlying each statement was SR's fear of being disciplined. Here, the record of trial shows that SR relied on Appellant to contain rumors that were circulating over what prosecutors cryptically referred to as her "bad situation" or "secret." (R. at 881, 901, 922- 23.) Both SR's "bad situation" and her encounter with Appellant in Chase Hall involved a military nexus that, if disclosed, subjected SR to discipline. Both incidents were connected, in that the encounter in Chase Hall
apparently was meant to secure Appellant's continued assistance in "suppressing" rumors regarding the earlier encounter.

I find it significant that the Government made first use of evidence of SR's secret during its case-in-chief. Although the prosecution was able to present evidence that SR was coerced into unwanted sexual relations with Appellant by the implied threat that he would reveal the facts of her "bad situation," the defense was prohibited from showing that this same fear of disclosure weighed so heavily in SR's mind that she relied on Appellant to disseminate false information concerning her secret. The anomalous result was that the members heard only the Government's evidence on the question of SR's motivation in submit- ting to Appellant's advances, while the defense was un- able to complete the picture by showing the depths of her fear and the lengths she allegedly had gone—and was prepared to go—to shield the facts of her misconduct.

I disagree that the cross-examination allowed the defense was adequate to develop SR's motive to testify falsely against Appellant. The sexual encounter between SR and Appellant had many outward appear ances of being consensual. The Government's case of indecent assault was not strong and turned on the members finding the existence of coercion that was sufficient to overcome the victim's will. Resolving this is- sue necessarily required the members to carefully evaluate the potentially subtle psychological pressure that resulted from Appellant's veiled threat to reveal the truth about SR's secret—a threat that Appellant denied making. Certainly, one explanation for SR's en- counter with Appellant was that she felt coerced into unwanted sexual relations. Another entirely plausible explanation was that the encounter resulted from her own calculation that Appellant needed additional "motivation" to continue spreading false information on her behalf.[1] Both scenarios would account for the consider- able pressure SR was under after Appellant informed her that rumors still were circulating about her secret, but the latter would not necessarily describe extortion or an indecent assault.[2] Appellant could not develop this alternate scenario at trial because he was prohibited from adequately addressing SR's prior false statement.

In addition, the Government offered no evidence of a fresh complaint and no other evidence to support SR's

---

[1] The defense attempted to develop this alternate theory during cross-examination of SR, but was hamstrung by its inability to speak directly to the facts of the prior false allegation. (R. at 903.)

[2] In fact, the Government, in apparent acknowledgment of the subtle psychological pressures at work, responsibly determined that it would not charge Appellant with forcible sodomy. In its answer and brief, the Government explained, "[a]s a practical matter, it would be difficult to convict someone of forcible sodomy on these facts, however, that does not mean that the conduct was con- sensual." (Government Br. 7.)

account of the incident involving Appellant.

SR was the Government's key witness against Appellant—in fact, SR's testimony was the only evidence supporting Appellant's conviction on extortion and indecent assault. Moreover, her own testimony on the question of consent was far from conclusive. For example, al-though SR testified that at one point during their en- counter she pushed Appellant's head aside and told him, "Please don't," she also testified that they kissed each other and exchanged back massages; that he told her, "You don't have to if you don't want to"; and that she thanked him for his support—presumably in reference to his assistance in defusing rumors regarding her secret. (R. at 885-86, 889-92, 914-17.) On the unusual facts of this case, it was essential that the defense be given wide latitude to explore SR's credibility, and to fully develop any motive reasonably raised by the evidence that she would bring a false allegation of sexual assault against Appellant. *See Moss*, 63 M.J. at 236 ("rules of evidence should be read to allow liberal ad- mission of bias-type evidence").

The members eventually did hear SR admit that her secret involved a violation of Cadet Regulations (R. at 899), and that she had misled Appellant about the circumstances, saying, "Yes, I did lie to him" (R. at 901). In addition, defense counsel argued in closing that SR "admitted she lied to Cadet Smith." (R. at 1510.) This limited impeachment allowed the defense was in- adequate given that a general attack on a witness'
credibility is not the same as a showing of bias or mo-tive. *See Davis*, 415 U.S. at 316-[566]17.

Here, the members never were able to place SR's admission that she had lied to Appellant in any factual context, be- cause they never heard what the secret was or what she had lied about. The members only heard that SR

223

had lied to Appellant in the past, not why she would have lied in bringing allegations against Appellant.

More importantly, SR was able to minimize her lie to Appellant by testifying that she had only omitted certain details from her account, saying, "I just didn't tell him all that occurred," and also that she told him, "I'm not gonna ask you to lie for me." (R. at 902-03.) Her testimony on this point created a substantially different impression of her credibility than what the defense had tried to show—namely, that SR had knowingly provided Appellant with false information, which he then used to counter a career-threatening rumor. *See Olden v. Kentucky*, 488 U.S. 227, 232 (1988) (defendant states a violation of Confrontation Clause if a "reasonable jury might have received a significantly different impression of [the witness'] credibility" had excluded line of cross-examination been allowed). Establishing this point was essential, as the crux of Appellant's defense was that SR had followed a pattern of fabrication to avoid discipline that was revealed by like motives from a prior scheme. Given this record, where SR was able to downplay her lie as a mere omission of details, and the defense was not allowed to inform the members what SR had lied about or the lengths she was prepared to go to protect her career, the members may well have concluded that the defense was engaged in a "speculative and baseless line of attack on the credibility of an apparently blameless witness." *Davis*, 415 U.S. at 318.

The military judge issued his ruling under M.R.E. 412, which broadly prohibits the introduction of evidence of a victim's past sexual behavior or sexual pre-disposition, unless the evidence fits into one of three

224

narrow exceptions.[3] Appellant moved to admit the facts of SR's secret under M.R.E. 412(b)(1)(C), which provides an exception for "evidence the exclusion of which would violate the constitutional rights of the accused."[4] Evidence that is offered under an enumerated exception to M.R.E. 412 shall be admitted if the military judge determines that the evidence is relevant and that the probative value outweighs the danger of unfair prejudice—i.e., prejudice to the privacy interests of the alleged victim. *See* M.R.E. 412(c)(3); *United States v. Sanchez*, 44 M.J. 174, 178 (C.A.A.F. 1996). In addition, relevant evidence that is offered under the constitutionally required exception must be admitted if it is material and favorable to the defense, and therefore is necessary. *United States v. Banker*, 60 M.J. 216, 222 (C.A.A.F. 2004).

---

[3] M.R.E. 412 is modeled after Federal Rule of Evidence 412 and is intended to protect victims of sexual offenses from degrad- ing and embarrassing disclosure of intimate details of their private lives while preserving the constitutional rights of the accused to present a defense. Appendix 22 at A22-36, Manual for Courts- Martial, United States (2005 ed.).

[4] I agree with the majority that the trial defense team did not precisely address the admissibility of the evidence in terms of SR's "motive" to fabricate. Indeed, it appears that the defense objec- tion has assumed greater clarity and focus on appeal. The defense, however, did argue at trial that the evidence implicated Appel- lant's confrontation rights to show the witness's "biases and … credibility," in that it revealed SR's "pattern" of claiming that pro- hibited consensual relations were coerced when disclosure could be damaging to her career. (R. at 97-98.) By focusing on SR's con- scious decision to lie under similar circumstances in order to avoid punishment, the defense adequately raised the issue of SR's mo- tive to fabricate allegations against Appellant.

In a detailed ruling, the military judge correctly determined that evidence of a prior false claim of sexual assault was relevant evidence of SR's motive to make a false claim of indecent assault against Appellant, stating, "I agree that this theory would be a valid reason for admitting this evidence under M.R.E. 412(b)(1)(C)
...." (Appellate Ex. **CLIII** at 3.)

The military judge reasoned:

[I]f the members hear that [SR] originally told Cadet Smith that a sexual encounter with an- other man was non-consensual, and then later admitted that it in fact was consensual, then the members could ... infer that the same thing is happening in this case. *Id.*
However, the military judge then went on to con-
clude that the evidence had "low" probative value be- cause:

[567] [T]he evidence proffered that [SR] made these statements is not strong since it comes from the accused, who has an obvious bias. [SR]'s written statement and Article 32 testi mony on this point is not clear. She admitted at the Article 32 that she only partially confided in Cadet Smith in May and fully confided in him on October 19th; however, this is far from proof that she initially claimed that the encounter was non-consensual.

In fact, it is consistent with the rest of Cadet Smith's Article 39(a) testimony that on October 19th she told him the scope of the sexual encounter had been greater than she had previously described. *Id.*

I would find that the military judge erred when he decided the probative value of motive evidence based on his evaluation of the credibility of the only two wit- nesses involved. It is the members' role to determine whether a witness' testimony is credible or biased. *Bins*, 43 M.J. at 85. "In applying M.R.E. 412, the judge is not asked to determine if the proffered evidence is true; it is for the members to weigh the evidence and determine its veracity." *Banker*, 60 M.J. at 224. Accordingly, relevant and material evidence of a prior false allegation of sexual assault is no less admissible merely because it is offered through the testimony of the criminal accused.

This is particularly so here, where SR—the only other witness to the conversation in issue—secured her unavailability to testify at the motions hearing by invoking her rights against self- incrimination.[5] (R. at 79.) In a credibility contest be- tween Appellant and SR, it should have been up to the members to resolve discrepancies in their respective accounts and decide whom to believe.

As a second basis for excluding the defense evi- dence, the military judge concluded that SR's state-

---

[5] Because SR refused to testify, the military judge based his findings on Appellant's in-court testimony, SR's prior written statement, and the non-verbatim summary of her Article 32 testimony. Based on my review of the complete record, I would find that there was at least a reasonable probability that SR provided Appellant with a false account of her secret— namely that the en- counter was non-consensual—which he then used to counter rumors on her behalf. Appellant's testimony concerning their initial conversation was partially corroborated in several key respects by SR's trial testimony, including her admission that the conversation took place, that she had "lied" to Appellant by omitting details that presented her in a "bad light," and that Appellant had assisted her by "squashing" rumors of her secret. (R. at 878, 901-02.)

ment to Appellant was materially different from a re- port that she subsequently provided to investigators. The military judge stated:

[E]ven if [SR] falsely told the accused *in confidence* that her sexual encounter with the enlisted man was non-consensual *in an effort to suppress rumors*, this would have little value in proving that her *official* allegations against Cadet Smith *resulting in a public trial* are also false.

(Appellate Ex. CLIII at 3.)

The military judge then concluded, "[T]he minimal probative value of this evidence is outweighed by danger of unfair prejudice to [SR's] privacy interests and the potential danger of sidetracking the member's [sic] attention to a collateral issue ...." *Id.*

In a trial on charges of extortion and coerced sexual relations, I do not agree that the defense intrudes in a collateral matter by making an inquiry into facts that describe the victim's fear that her secret will be revealed. Proof of the secret's existence and the genuineness of SR's fear of disclosure were key issues in the Government's case against Appellant, and the defense had a right to explore them, subject to carefully tailored restrictions respecting SR's privacy.[6] Moreover,

---

[6] The military judge clearly recognized the relevance of the content of the secret to the extortion and indecent assault offenses, observing, "[I]f the secret is about something that is completely inconsequential, it makes it less likely that [SR] would have been willing to do something against her will." (R. at 112.) Ultimately, however, the Government was able to prove both the existence and importance of the secret through the witness's layering on of additional conclusory statements.

by focusing on the confidential versus official nature of SR's two statements, the military judge overlooked the greater significance of the defense proffer. The defense theory was that SR's ultimate motive in avoiding discipline was revealed in her expectation that Appellant would place his reputation on the line and communicate false information to counter rumors then in circulation about her secret.[7] The defense argued that [568] this same motive was also present in her complaint against Appellant, and it seems an artificial distinction to say that the formality of the complaint process somehow altered SR's overriding concern for protecting her career. *Compare United States v. Bahr*, 33 M.J. 228, 233 (C.M.A. 1991) (error to exclude evidence of witness' prior false statements to classmates that she had been sexually assaulted; evidence was admissible to show witness' motive to testify falsely against accused in order to call attention to herself).

The majority largely sidesteps the problems with the M.R.E. 412 order and under its Article 66(c), Uniform Code of Military Justice (UCMJ), authority concludes that the instant case involves non-parallel statements—an earlier statement to Appellant where avoiding discipline was a factor in SR's motivation to lie, and a second statement to law enforcement investi-

---

[7] There is no dispute that SR did not actively seek out Appellant to lie for her concerning her secret. However, after furnishing Appellant with an allegedly false account of her secret, SR apparently did nothing to discourage Appellant from using that information to counter rumors that were in circulation. In fact, SR's approval of Appellant's efforts to "help her" by suppressing rumors was reflected in her own trial testimony (R. at 901, 922-23, 926), and Appellant's threatened withholding of that assistance ultimately formed the basis of the Government's extortion charge.

else knew about the encounter and SR had no reason to fear UCMJ action.

The majority emphatically concludes that because SR had no possible motive to fabricate her allegations against Appellant, the earlier statement was not relevant and therefore was inadmissible at trial.

The flaw in the majority's argument is the implicit assumption that no circumstances other than the *actual disclosure* of the facts surrounding the Chase Hall encounter could have provided SR with the motive to fabricate allegations of sexual assault. In my view, the timing, content, and circumstances surround- ing SR's initial report to investigators all point to the making of an intrinsically unreliable statement, and provide sufficient grounds to question SR's motives in bringing her allegations against Appellant.

The record reveals that on 5 December 2005, Coast Guard Investigative Service (CGIS) agents inter- viewed Appellant—the other person who knew of the Chase Hall encounter—as part of a large-scale probe into allegations of his sexual misconduct at the Coast Guard Academy. SR was not interviewed by CGIS until almost two months later, on 9 February 2006,[8] at which time she discussed her allegations against Appellant but specifically refused to address the details of her secret. SR's self-censored initial report reveals that she had made the gators where no such motive existed because nobody understandable but nevertheless calculated decision to limit the disclosure of information that could be harmful to her career.[9] Such a decision on

----

[8] The record does not disclose whether SR voluntarily came forward or was first approached by CGIS.

[9] In her signed statement to CGIS dated 15 February 2006, SR also indicated, "A situation occurred, that I do not which [sic]

SR's part following a considerable opportunity for reflection necessarily calls into question the completeness and reliability of her contemporaneous allegations against Appellant. Given the visibility of this dragnet investigation, the four-month delay between the Chase Hall encounter and SR's initial report, and her selective and continued withholding of facts that did not reflect favorably on her, it certainly was possible that SR fabricated or embellished details of her allegation against Appellant as a preemptive strike to avoid discipline, based on *her fear or expectation* that the true facts of their encounter, if not already known by investigators, likely would be discovered.[10] Accordingly, the two statements were "parallel" not because anyone else knew the facts, but because of the illegality of the encounters and SR's fear that the true facts *could be* discovered. Whether or not SR actually formed the motive to fabricate allegations against Appellant was an

---

to discuss, which led to rumors (which were grossly exaggerated)." (Appellate Ex. **XVII**, Enclosure 13 at 1; Appellate Ex. **XXI** at 2.) SR's clear attempt to downplay the rumors while at the same time refusing to address them indicates, in my mind at least, a concern for UCMJ or administrative action, if not a desire to deflect official interest in her own behavior.

[10] Given the ongoing CGIS investigation, there certainly would have been risks to SR in not stepping forward at all. SR likely had no way of knowing if Appellant had already reported their encounter to CGIS agents, leaving the possibility of an unrebutted, potentially career-threatening allegation of sexual misconduct in the hands of authorities. There also was the risk that Appellant might decide to cooperate with authorities and make a pre- emptive disclosure at a future time. The argument that the record completely foreclosed the possibility of fabrication by SR would make more sense if SR had made a prompt and complete report of her allegations against Appellant at a time prior to the CGIS investigation. That did not happen in this case

issue that that the members should have decided at trial.

Faced with a recalcitrant key witness who refused to testify at the motions hearing, the Government obtained a windfall through the erroneous application of M.R.E. 412.

At trial, SR provided conclusory testimony regarding her "bad situation" and Appellant's prior role in "squashing" career-threatening rumors, for the purpose of showing that she was coerced into unwanted sexual relations after Appellant impliedly threatened to reveal the truth about her secret.

On cross-examination, the defense was prohibited from ad- dressing the facts of SR's "bad situation" or "secret," and similarly was prohibited from eliciting factual testimony that would inform the members that Appellant's efforts to "squash" and "suppress" rumors specifically meant spreading false information provided by SR, on SR's behalf.[11] The result was that the Government was allowed to portray SR as an innocent victim of an extortionist plot, while the defense was not al- lowed to portray the witness as the architect of a scheme of false allegations intended to cover up her own misconduct. I cannot agree that SR's privacy interest in shielding her alleged false statements from inquiry was so important that it justified denying Ap- pellant the opportunity to pierce the veneer of the Gov- ernment's conclusory assertions that were used to con- vict him. I disagree with the notion that M.R.E. 412 was intended to allow the Government to prove the *corpus delicti* of the offenses through a witness indulging in euphemisms of doubtful legal sufficiency, particu-

---

[11] The record of trial is devoid of any facts that would have explained to the members what these words actually meant.

larly when they obscure facts that raise serious questions concerning her own credibility.[12]

When a constitutional violation is shown, a case must be reversed unless the error is harmless beyond a reasonable doubt. *United States v. Israel*, 60 M.J. 485, 488 (C.A.A.F. 2005). In deciding whether or not the erroneous exclusion of evidence is harmless, the court must consider "the importance of the witness' testimony in the prosecution's case, whether the testimony was cumulative, the presence or absence of evidence corroborating or contradicting the testimony of the witness on materials points, the extent of cross- examination otherwise permitted, and ... the strength of the prosecution's case." *United States v. Moss*, 63 M.J. 233, 238 (C.A.A.F. 2006) (*quoting Bahr*, 33 M.J. 228 at 234 (quoting *Delaware v. Van Arsdall*, 465 U.S. 673, 684 (1986))). At trial, SR testified that on 19 October 2005, she had discussed her secret with Appellant in the mailroom; that Appellant had responded by indicating he needed "motivation" to keep "helping her" by
continuing to suppress rumors that were circulating about her; that she had replied by asking whether by "motivation" he meant sex—a suggestion she says

---

[12] Certainly there were less burdensome remedies available to the military judge that could have protected the legitimate privacy interests of the victim in this case. The military judge could have fashioned an order restricting the defense from probing the intimate and personal details of the secret, focusing instead on the nature of the encounter and the alleged false claim of sexual assault. In addition, the military judge could have closed the pro- ceeding during testimony on the May 2005 incident to protect the victim from undue embarrassment or humiliation. The military judge also could have provided instructions to the members limit- ing the improper use of the evidence.

made him bristle; that Appellant later appeared in her room in Chase Hall on three separate occasions, where they posed together nude for a photograph and engaged in sexual activity; that the sexual encounter had in her mind provided the "motivation" Appellant needed to continue to suppress her secret; and that al- though she never told Appellant to stop, she participated only out of fear that he would not keep her secret.

Appellant presented his case upon his own testi mony, stating in substance that while he met SR in the mailroom on 19 October, he never extorted sexual favors from her and denied saying that he needed "motivation" to continue suppressing rumors about SR's secret. Appellant testified that they discussed get- ting together to pose for a nude photograph in her room; that after arriving in her room that evening, he took two digital photographs of them together, which he kept for safekeeping; and that he subsequently re- turned to her room on two additional occasions to ex- change massages and perform consensual oral sodomy. Appellant admitted that SR was "tense" and "stressed" but claimed that the entire sexual encounter with SR was consensual. (R. at 1325.)

The difficulty accepting Appellant's account of a consensual encounter with SR is that it makes little intuitive sense given the lack of any evidence of a relationship or any rational explanation for its spontaneous nature. In short, Appellant's testimony is remarkable in its failure to explain SR's actions in the absence of at least some undue influence. In this failure, however, lies the major flaw in the military judge's M.R.E. 412 order.

Appellant's account of an almost spontaneous consensual encounter with SR would be difficult to believe unless the members were informed of SR's prior false claim and were able to understand the depths of her concern for protecting her career. Only if informed of SR's prior scheme would the members have considered the possibility that her encounter with Appellant in October 2005 resulted not so much from coercion, but rather from her own calculation that she needed to en- sure his continued cooperation in keeping her prior misconduct secret. Only then would the members have considered the possibility that SR might have fabricated a false claim of sexual assault against Appellant as a preemptive strike, out of fear that the encounter would be discovered through an ongoing investigation. The erroneous M.R.E. 412 order deprived Appellant of his best defense to the charges involving SR.

See United States v. Gray, 40 M.J. 77, 80 (C.M.A. 1994) (military judge committed reversible error by excluding evidence of victim's past sexual behavior under M.R.E. 412; case came down to a credibility contest between witnesses, and the excluded evidence "could have made [the accused's] otherwise incredible explanation believable"); *see also United States v. Williams,*
37 M.J. 352, 360 (C.M.A. 1993) (accused's constitutional right to present evidence of victim's extramarital affair improperly excluded under M.R.E. 412; excluded evidence would have revealed motive to provide false testimony in order to protect affair, victim was key witness in government's case, and evidence of guilt was not overwhelming).

Here, the Government offered no other evidence to support SR's testimony that her sexual encounter with Appellant, which had many outward indicators of being consensual, actually resulted from coercion.
The ad- mission of evidence that SR had furnished Appellant with false information which he then used to counter a career-threatening rumor may well have cast doubt on

the veracity of SR's testimony, and tipped the balance in favor of Appellant's version of events. Accordingly, **I** would find that the error in excluding this evidence was not harmless beyond a reasonable doubt.

I would affirm the findings of guilty to sodomy, at- tempted failure to obey a lawful order, and unauthorized absence. **I** would set aside the findings of guilty to extortion and indecent assault, and the sentence, and return the case to the Convening Authority for a rehearing.

For the Court,

Jane R. Lee
Clerk of the Court

APPENDIX 8

Decision of Supreme Court Without Comment Denying Certiorari

IN THE SUPREME COURT OF THE UNITED STATES OF
AMERICA
No. 10-18
Title:**Webster M. Smith**, Petitioner
v.
United States
Docketed:June 30, 2010
Lower Ct:United States Court of Appeals for the Armed Forces
Case Nos.:(08-0719)
Decision Date:March 29, 2010
Date ~~~ Proceedings and Orders

Jun 28 2010 Petition for a writ of certiorari filed. (Response due July 30, 2010)

Jul 21 2010 Order extending time to file response to petition to and including August 30, 2010.

Jul 30 2010 Brief amicus curiae of National Association of Criminal Defense Lawyers filed.

Jul 30 2010 Brief amicus curiae of United States Army Defense Appellate Division filed.

Aug 23 2010 Order further extending time to file response to petition to and including September 29, 2010.

Sep 22 2010 Order further extending time to file response to petition to and including October 28, 2010.

Oct 28 2010 Brief of respondent United States in opposition filed.

Nov 5 2010 Reply of petitioner Webster M. Smith filed. TBP

Nov 8 2010 DISTRIBUTED for Conference of November 23, 2010.

Nov 29 2010 Petition DENIED.

Name~~~~~~~~~~~~~~~~~ Address~~~~~~~~~~~~~~~~Phone~~~

Attorneys for Petitioner:

Daniel S. Volchok, Wilmer Cutler Hale and Dorr LLP(202) 663-6000

1875 Pennsylvania Avenue, NW

Washington, DC 20006

Party name: Webster M. Smith

Attorneys for Respondent:

Neal Kumar Katyal, <u>Acting Solicitor General</u>(202) 514-2217

United States Department of Justice

950 Pennsylvania Avenue, N.W.

Washington, DC 20530-0001

SupremeCtBriefs@USDOJ

Party name: United States

Other:

Jonathan L. Marcus, Covington & Burling, LLP(202) 662-6000

1201 Pennsylvania Avenue, NW

Washington, DC 20004

jmarcus@cov.com

Party name: National Association of Criminal Defense Lawyers

Jonathan F. Potter, Senior Appellate Counsel United States Army(703) 588-6717

Defense Appellate Division

901 N. Stuart Street

Arlington, VA 22203

jonathan.potter@conus.army.mil

Party name: United States Army Defense Appellate Division

APPENDIX 9

Emails Sent From KN and KS to Webster Smith

Kristen's screen name is <u>swim113mer.</u> This was one of Brittney's screen names at the time milkgonebad09

Check out the date, and of course now we know that was Kristen. From the beginning of this, Kristen told us, "<u>I have nothing to do with this</u>." At first, we believed her, I gave these emails to the Defense Attorneys to present in court to show that she also defied Wisnewski's orders and they did nothing with them. They were able to use emails by Kristen's friend "<u>Jersey</u>" to convict Webster, yet Merle and Kirkby neglected to do the same. If the court had known she was contacting us when she was told not to talk to anyone, it could have made a bigger impact on the charge of attempting to disobey an officer.

Date: 12/29/2005 7:16:35 PM Central Standard Time

Swim113mer: i am trying to be ok. your family hates me and i wish everyone would just be on the same page

Swim113mer: i don't know what is going on and <u>i am not supposed to contact anyone</u>

Swim113mer: my phone is broken

BSMITH2524: no way do we hate

Swim113mer: i cry a lot

Swim113mer: and your daughter thinks i forgot about him

Swim113mer: and you guys

BSMITH2524: she's just concerned

Swim113mer: webster took me off his list of friends on facebook and brittney thinks i did it

Swim113mer: i am concerned

Swim113mer: <u>i am not supposed to speak to anyone</u>

Swim113mer: i haven't spoken to anyone from school

239

Swim113mer: i don't even know what is going on

BSMITH2524: i know and he didn't do that it was a mistake when britatney was sonj

BSMITH2524: he thought you took him off

Swim113mer: ms. smith i am not allowed to talk to anyone

Swim113mer: i am isolated

Swim113mer: no i didn't

Swim113mer: i would never do that

Swim113mer: i am not like that

Swim113mer: i am no different than before

BSMITH2524: ok you take care of yourself

Swim113mer: i hate this

Swim113mer: i hope you are all okay

BSMITH2524: i know

Swim113mer: 1 year ago i was getting ready to come to Texas

BSMITH2524: and i put your stocking on the tree this year too

Swim113mer: this hurts

Swim113mer: yea

Swim113mer: i am sorry i cannot talk

Swim113mer: maybe after everything is over we can more

BSMITH2524: i know and i agree

Swim113mer: i haven't forgotten

BSMITH2524: i know

Swim113mer: so much i need to know

Swim113mer: find out the truth

Swim113mer: i am completely blindsighted by a lot

BSMITH2524: give my love to your parents

BSMITH2524: so are we

Swim113mer: happy new year to you guys

BSMITH2524: you too ! God Bless you

Swim113mer: webster hates me.

Swim113mer: i can't talk to him

BSMITH2524: he will never

240

Swim113mer: i don't understand why this happened
Swim113mer: i will never forget
BSMITH2524: he doesn't talk about it
BSMITH2524: he loves you
Swim113mer: i don't think anyone will ever love him like i do
Swim113mer: ms. smith
Swim113mer: please have a happy new year
Swim113mer: keep him safe
BSMITH2524: same to you i will
Swim113mer: i will never ever forget
Swim113mer: but when people question me
Swim113mer: i have to do as i am told
Swim113mer: and i am just really sad
Swim113mer: have a good night. i am sorry that i cannot talk . but it will hurt both of us if we do.
Swim113mer: i have to follow their orders.
Swim113mer: happy new year.
BSMITH2524: do not talk then ok
Swim113mer: i would never hurt him
BSMITH2524: happy new year....sushi this year:-)
Swim113mer: you're going to have sushi
Swim113mer: ? i bet it will be wonderful
BSMITH2524: remember last year
Swim113mer: ill be with the family.
Swim113mer: how could i forget.
Swim113mer: have a good night
Swim113mer: god bless
BSMITH2524: Good night and God bless you too!

Sent: Mon, Feb 6, 2006 1:57 pm
Subject: Fwd: here...When Kris contacted Brittney
Swim113mer: kris is asleep
Swim113mer: this is her friend

241

MilksGoneBad09: oh hi

Swim113mer: she gets sad sometimes

MilksGoneBad09: i bet

Swim113mer: a lot of times

MilksGoneBad09: so does web

MilksGoneBad09: its kinda pathetic

Swim113mer: don't ever tell her i got on

MilksGoneBad09: i won't

Swim113mer: she let me use her computer for hw

MilksGoneBad09: oh

Swim113mer: he hates her

MilksGoneBad09: omg

Swim113mer: <u>and she loved him more than life itself</u>

MilksGoneBad09: that is a live

MilksGoneBad09: lie*

Swim113mer: she knows he has a new gf

MilksGoneBad09: my brother cries to me all the time

MilksGoneBad09: because he can't have her...

Swim113mer: <u>adn she was lied to about a lot of things</u>

Swim113mer: she is a nice person

Swim113mer: she loves your family

MilksGoneBad09: i know

Swim113mer: she really cares about everything that comes in her path

MilksGoneBad09: he loves her a lot

Swim113mer: she will never believe it

Swim113mer: she doesn't believe in forever anymore

Swim113mer: she made me cry the other day

Swim113mer: on her birthday

MilksGoneBad09: i know that was their 2 year

MilksGoneBad09: he told me

Swim113mer: she said she hated forever and she hated her birthday

MilksGoneBad09: web is with that girl because he needs someone to lean on... and the person hes used to leaning on wasn't there for him

MilksGoneBad09: he loves her i know

MilksGoneBad09: like I'm not lying

MilksGoneBad09: i wouldn't

MilksGoneBad09: not about this

Swim113mer: its sick because when i ask her if she is mad at everything

Swim113mer: she isn't

Swim113mer: she only wanted him to be happy

MilksGoneBad09: me and my bro sat at chipotle for 3 hours talki0ng about kristin

MilksGoneBad09: for real

MilksGoneBad09: he went to Chicago a few weeks ago

MilksGoneBad09: and he all he saw was her kris's car

MilksGoneBad09: and he couldn't stop thinking about her

Swim113mer: she is a tough girl

Swim113mer: i don't know anything

Swim113mer: she won't talk

Swim113mer: but she is damn strong

MilksGoneBad09: well they said she said alot of bad things about him

MilksGoneBad09: and that hurts him

MilksGoneBad09: a lot

MilksGoneBad09: you have no idea

Swim113mer: i just hate when she cries

Swim113mer: they never use names

Swim113mer: I've been called down

MilksGoneBad09: well that's not what he heard

MilksGoneBad09: I'm sure he wouldn't make it up

MilksGoneBad09: he wants to be with kris i know

Swim113mer: special agents don't disclose names

MilksGoneBad09: but he thinks she said all this bad stuff and it doesn't make sense to him

MilksGoneBad09: and he wants to know why she would hurt him like that

Swim113mer: she would never hurt him

Swim113mer: ever

Swim113mer: she got called down

Swim113mer: i was with her that night

Swim113mer: she got called down out of nowhere

Swim113mer: took her stuff

Swim113mer: and now she is not allowed to talk

MilksGoneBad09: yeah

MilksGoneBad09: i know that

Swim113mer: she didn't do anything. now she is forced to answer questions

Swim113mer: but she won't talk

Swim113mer: and she is hurt

Swim113mer: and confused

Swim113mer: but she keeps it all in

Swim113mer: she thinks web hates her

MilksGoneBad09: january 13th was the hardest day my brother EVER had...

MilksGoneBad09: i know this

MilksGoneBad09: he loves her.

MilksGoneBad09: i promise

Swim113mer: she will never love anyone more than him.

Swim113mer: i think she is done.

Swim113mer: she is hurt too

Swim113mer: her family won't speak to her

MilksGoneBad09: the new girl will NEVER compare to kris

MilksGoneBad09: i know that

MilksGoneBad09: let her know that

MilksGoneBad09: please

Swim113mer: she will never know that know that

Swim113mer: no she will not believe me

MilksGoneBad09: he cant stop thinking about her

MilksGoneBad09: i wish i could prove it

MilksGoneBad09: i know my bro

Swim113mer: she doesn't think anyone deserves her. she doesn't believe in love anymore

MilksGoneBad09: he cries himself to sleep

Swim113mer: well she says that at least

MilksGoneBad09: im sorry about that

Swim113mer: she gets asked out and says no all the time

MilksGoneBad09: neither does he

Swim113mer: when i ask her why

Swim113mer: she just shrugs

MilksGoneBad09: wow...

MilksGoneBad09: that is really sad

MilksGoneBad09: there is one person there for wen

MilksGoneBad09: web

MilksGoneBad09: and he wants it to be kris

Swim113mer: she can't believe what has happened

MilksGoneBad09: he can't either

MilksGoneBad09: my bro is still in Houston

MilksGoneBad09: believe me

MilksGoneBad09: he can't either

Swim113mer: so just know that while webster is telling everyone that she did something that she did this or that

Swim113mer: she hasn't said a word

Swim113mer: she answers questions by interrogators

Swim113mer: she was hurt

Swim113mer: but never spoke

MilksGoneBad09: he's never said that

MilksGoneBad09: he thinks it on the inside

MilksGoneBad09: because he doesn't understand

Swim113mer: well neither does she

MilksGoneBad09: he doesn't even know what is going on

Swim113mer: neither does she

Swim113mer: she is rc here

Swim113mer: that's the person in charge of everything

245

Swim113mer: i don't know how she does it.
MilksGoneBad09: i try to get him to stop talking about her
MilksGoneBad09: but he doesn't
Swim113mer: i think it's the one thing that keeps her alive.
MilksGoneBad09: he doesn't hate her..
MilksGoneBad09: he wishes he could
MilksGoneBad09: because it would be easier
Swim113mer: she doesn't hate him
MilksGoneBad09: but I KNOW he doesn't
MilksGoneBad09: he's in love
MilksGoneBad09: i know
MilksGoneBad09: like hopelessly
Swim113mer: because she fell in love
Swim113mer: and now she's empty
Swim113mer: she just says
MilksGoneBad09: why can't she just be with him then?
Swim113mer: "as long as he is happy"
MilksGoneBad09: he's not thought
Swim113mer: I think there is more to it than we know
MilksGoneBad09: that's the point
MilksGoneBad09: I'm sure
Swim113mer: the truth will come out
MilksGoneBad09: hopefully
Swim113mer: but she does not lie
Swim113mer: she just wants the truth
MilksGoneBad09: so does
Swim113mer: she is glad he has a sister like you
Swim113mer: she has said that
Swim113mer: she has you under family, so i knew it had to be you
MilksGoneBad09: awwww
MilksGoneBad09: thats so sweet
Swim113mer: please don't tell her i spoke to you. i couldn't help it.
MilksGoneBad09: i wont promise

Swim113mer: sorry to interrupt you
MilksGoneBad09: its fine
Swim113mer: i guess i should finish my hw so i can get out of here
MilksGoneBad09: ok
Swim113mer: thank you for listening.
MilksGoneBad09: no problem
MilksGoneBad09: i love them both
Swim113mer: well he is your brother. but just know that she is a very real person
Swim113mer: who does not have the support he has from his family
MilksGoneBad09: i know
MilksGoneBad09: im praying for her
MilksGoneBad09: i know how that feels
MilksGoneBad09: its no good
MilksGoneBad09: im a girl too
Swim113mer: <u>she is also going through a lot of surguries and i don't know why</u>
Swim113mer: she won't tell me
Swim113mer: well i am glad that we have a common trait
Swim113mer: have a good night
MilksGoneBad09: you too
Swim113mer: i just needed to tell you that she doesn't hate him
Swim113mer: she doesn't hate anyone
Swim113mer: i am babbling sorry. i just wish i could help somehow and i can't
MilksGoneBad09: i know
Swim113mer: good night
MilksGoneBad09: good night
Swim113mer: is his away message about her
MilksGoneBad09: i don't think so...
Swim113mer: you didn't tell him you spoke to me did you
Swim113mer: she will die if she finds out
Swim113mer: please don't

MilksGoneBad09: i don't even get it

MilksGoneBad09: i won't

Swim113mer: i have to put her damn away message up now about perfection.

Swim113mer: this girl is too hopeful sometimes huh. she wants to be loved.

Swim113mer: thank you for listening again.

MilksGoneBad09: she is loved

MilksGoneBad09: I'm sorry she can't feel it

Swim113mer: she just thinks about him.

Swim113mer: gnite.

MilksGoneBad09: night

Swim113mer is away at 10:35:52 PM.

Swim113mer signed off at 10:36:04 PM.

Subject: 9 -13-2006 IM Message from Kristen

Swim113mer: Mrs. Smith?

Swim113mer: Mrs. Smith?

Swim113mer: I just wanted to say hello and let you know I am thinking of you -

Swim113mer: have a good night- i love you always - that will not change.

Swim113mer is away at 9:06 P.M.wil

Appendix 10

Initial Leaks To The Press From The CGA Public Information Office.

By RICHARD RAINEY

1/21/2006

New London,CT. The U.S. Coast Guard Academy has confirmed it is investigating a male cadet for an undisclosed number of sexual misconduct allegations filed against him in December.

The academy also disclosed this week that two other allegations of sexual misconduct were filed in the fall semester. One case resulted in the dismissal of a male cadet Dec. 15.

Chief Warrant Officer David French, an academy spokesman, declined to comment this week on the frequency or severity of the allegations in the latest case, or whether there are multiple complainants.

He said the Cadet Code of Regulations defines sexual misconduct as prohibited sexual behavior ranging from hand-holding to rape.

The academy investigations come at a time when other branches of the military are involved in a two-year effort to document and reduce the number of sexual assaults and incidents of harassment at their service academies.

The Coast Guard Academy largely limited its responses to The Day's questions to brief written statements delivered by e-mail. French declined a request by an editor and a reporter for an interview with Commandant of Cadets Capt. Douglas Wisniewski.

On Dec. 4, an officer on duty received an allegations of sexual misconduct from a cadet, setting off an inquiry by the Coast Guard Investigative Services, based in Washington, D.C., French said.

French declined to provide further details, citing the ongoing investigation.

Once its investigation is completed, and the results are reported to the academy, the command will make a determination whether further administrative or disciplinary action is warranted, French wrote of the latest case.

One of the other two complaints, stemming from the first semester of 2005-06, resulted in a confession and the Dec. 15 dismissal of a first-year male student, who departed immediately, according to French. He stated that a female cadet reported nonconsensual sexual advances from a freshman male in the Chase Hall barracks, the dormitory where all students reside.

No criminal charges have been filed, French said.

Capt. William D. Dittman of the New London Police Department said the department had not been contacted regarding the alleged incidents at the academy. Federal law enforcement agencies have primary jurisdiction at the campus. City police have authority over specific areas there, he explained, but not the barracks.

Cmdr. Kathleen Donohoe of the Coast Guard's national public affairs office in Washington, D.C. declined to comment, citing the ongoing investigation. A phone call to the regional office of the internal investigative services unit in Boston was not returned.

In 2003, women's reports of a number of incidents involving sexual misconduct at the Air Force Academy spurred Congress, through the 2004 Defense Authorization legislation, to order an examination of the prevalence of sexual harassment and violence in service academies.

The same legislation created a task force to survey the frequency of sexual assaults at the U.S. military and naval academies. The task force visited the Coast Guard Academy sometime between September 2004 and June 2005, according to an Aug. 25 defense department briefing.

In December, the Defense Department released the Service Academy 2005 Sexual Harassment And Assault Survey. The Air Force Academy showed marked improvement, with about 4 percent of women acknowledging incidents of sexual assault during the 2004-05 school year, a number slightly lower than those reported at the naval and military academies.

No statistics on the Coast Guard Academy were included in the defense department's survey. The Coast Guard operates under the U.S. Department of Homeland Security.

Appendix 11

The Coast Guard Academy is investigating a male cadet on allegations of sexual misconduct.

The inquiry, first reported Jan. 21 by The Day newspaper of New London, Conn., involves at least one charge of misconduct by the student. A complaint was filed against him Dec. 4 with the school's chain of command, prompting the Coast Guard Investigative Service to look into the allegations.

The case is the school's third sexual misconduct investigation this academic year. In the first, a male cadet fourth class admitted to making unsolicited sexual advances toward a female cadet at Chase Hall, the academy's student barracks. He was dismissed from the school Dec. 15.

An investigation into the second incident is pending, academy spokesman Chief Warrant Officer 2 Dave French said Jan. 24.
French declined to give details of the latest case, citing the ongoing inquiry. At the Coast Guard Academy, if a report involving sexual assault or misconduct is made to the chain of command, CGIS must examine it.
"The commandant of cadets, Capt. Douglas Wisniewski, took immediate action to initiate the investigation into these allegations", French said.

"Sexual misconduct" at the academy is defined as "acts that disgrace or bring discredit on the Coast Guard or Coast Guard Academy and are sexual in nature", including lewd or lascivious acts, indecent exposure or homosexual conduct.

But the definition also includes consensual acts that are prohibited on academy grounds, such as holding hands, kissing in public or sex.

The Coast Guard cases come a year after Congress required the Defense Department to examine the problem of sexual harassment and violence at its service academies. A Defense Department survey released in March 2005 revealed that nearly one in seven women at the service academies "the Naval Academy, the U.S Military Academy at West Point and the Air Force Academy " said they were sexually assaulted during their college careers. More than half said they were subjected to sexual harassment.

The Coast Guard is not a Defense Department armed service, and its academy was not part of the survey, but the Defense Department task force assigned to study the problem visited the academy Jan. 11, 2005, to "gain an understanding of our programs and policies and how our system of reporting differs from the other service academies", French said.

From 1993 until the spring semester of 2005, the Coast Guard had 10 reported incidents of sexual misconduct, according to information provided by the academy. Of those, six incidents resulted in dismissal of the accused and two ended in resignation. In the remaining two cases, there was insufficient evidence to pursue charges.

The Coast Guard Academy has 982 students, nearly 30 percent of whom are women.

From 2000 to 2003, the Naval Academy reported investigating 13 incidents of sexual misconduct. Of those, at least four were substantiated and resulted in punitive actions against the midshipmen involved. The Naval Academy has about 4,300 students.

The Air Force Academy, whose widespread problems came to light in 2003, triggering the dismissal of much of that school's leadership and prompting Congressional inquiries, had 54 incidents between 1993 and 2003.

The rates of assaults and harassment found by the Defense Department survey mirror similar results of surveys done at civilian colleges and universities.

But the military services aim to uphold a higher standard, said Naval Academy Superintendent Vice Adm. Rodney Rempt in a press release following the release of the Defense Department task force's final report in August 2005.

"The public trusts that the service academies will adhere to the highest standards and that we will serve as beacons that exemplify character, dignity and respect. We will increase our efforts to meet that trust", Rempt said.

Appendix 12

Coast Guard Cadet Charged With Rape

Associated Press | February 17, 2006

NEW LONDON, Conn. - A senior at the U.S. Coast Guard Academy has been charged with sexually assaulting six female cadets in the campus barracks and other sites.

Webster M. Smith, 22, of Houston was separated from the rest of the student population after the first complaint was filed with administrators Dec. 4, the academy said.

Smith, a linebacker on the academy's football team, was charged Feb. 9 under military law with rape, assault, indecent assault and sodomy against female cadets, said Chief Warrant Officer David French, an academy spokesman.

Some of the attacks allegedly happened on academy grounds when Smith entered female cadets' rooms without permission. Others were reported off campus. The rape allegedly occurred in June 2005 during a trip to Annapolis, French said.

A military hearing was tentatively scheduled for March 15 to determine whether there is enough evidence for a trial that could result in a court-martial, French said. Such a military hearing is typically open to the public, but the presiding military official could close it.

After the hearing, the academy's superintendent, Rear Adm. James C. Van Sice, will decide how to proceed.

While separated from other cadets, Smith was not jailed and was allowed to return home for holiday leave. He returned to campus Tuesday and was assigned a work area on academy grounds along the waterfront, an area other cadets are prohibited from entering, the academy said.

"He's no longer in the barracks, and he does not actually stay at the campus at night," French said.

Smith's lawyer, Merle Smith, who is not related, told WTIC-TV the cadet insists he is not guilty of all charges.

"The public is only receiving one side of the story, as all of the charges in their most sordid representation," the lawyer said.

It was unclear whether the alleged victims were under Smith's military command, although seniors have supervisory power over lower-level cadets. French would not release the women's class ranks.

French said there is no recent record of any previous courts-martial at the academy, the smallest federal service academy, with about 980 cadets. About 280 are women, according to its Web site. Male and female cadets share dormitories but have separate rooms.

In 2004, nearly 150 women at the Air Force Academy in Colorado came forward with accusations that they had been sexually assaulted by fellow cadets between 1993 and 2003. Many alleged they were ignored or ostracized by commanders for speaking out. A Pentagon task force found that hostile attitudes and inappropriate treatment of women also persisted at the U.S. Military Academy at West Point and at the Naval Academy.

Appendix 13

Other Cases Of Alleged Sexual Misconduct Had Been Handled Differently -- Cadet Kicked Out Instead of Prosecuted

Associated Press | February 25, 2006

NEW LONDON, Conn. - A prosecutor said he's reviewing how information is exchanged with the U.S. Coast Guard Academy after learning a cadet who admitted sexual misconduct wasn't prosecuted but kicked out of school last year.

New London State's Attorney Kevin Kane would not say whether he believes he has jurisdiction in the case at the academy in this coastal Connecticut city.

An academy spokesman said he could not comment on the case, citing privacy rules.

"It was fully investigated and handled appropriately," Chief Warrant Officer David French said Friday.

According to an academy discipline summary, the male cadet was expelled in December after admitting to sexual misconduct that was determined to be nonconsensual.

"This case has precipitated a review of our policies and procedures with regard to our jurisdictional boundaries, our communication and our respective responsibilities," Kane said. "I have no reason to believe we're not on the same page."

In an interview this week, Capt. Douglas Wisniewski, the commandant of cadets, said the Coast Guard Investigative Service investigated the woman's assault claims. He would not discuss specifics but said prosecution requires more evidence than needed for academy disciplinary decisions.

The woman received medical treatment in October, hospital records show.

Last week, a senior at the academy was charged by the military with raping or assaulting six classmates. The cadet, who has denied any wrongdoing, would be the first sexual assault court martial in the academy's history.

Appendix 14

The Article 32 Investigation Begins. Coast Guard Cadets' Rape Hearing Begins

Associated Press | March 21, 2006

NEW LONDON, Connecticut - A U.S. Naval Academy midshipman testified Tuesday about a night of heavy drinking with two Coast Guard cadets that ended with one accusing the other of rape. Midshipman Kristin Strizki was among the final witnesses for the government at a hearing that will determine whether Coast Guard Cadet Webster M. Smith, 22, a member of the academy football team, is court-martialed.

Seven female cadets have accused Smith of assaulting them between May and November 2005. One of the cadets, a friend of Strizki's, said she was raped.

The woman was among five alleged victims who testified Monday in secret at the Article 32 hearing, the military equivalent of a grand jury. Strizki's testimony Tuesday was public.

Strizki said that the two Coast Guard cadets were visiting her in Annapolis, Maryland, when they began drinking at an off-campus house. She said the alleged victim passed out after consuming more than 2 liters of wine and two beers.

The next morning, Smith suggested Strizki take her friend to get the morning-after pill, she said.

Strizki said her friend had no recollection of having sex with Smith and confronted him.

"He said, 'Oh please, you wanted it,'" she testified. "That's when she said, 'There is no way in hell I would have wanted to have sex with you last night, even if I was sober.'"

Another witness, Coast Guard cadet Jere Cherni, testified that the alleged victim became pregnant and underwent an operation that she felt was immoral. After objections from Smith's attorneys, Cherni was not permitted to specify the operation.

Smith's attorney, Lt. Stuart Kirkby, said his client is innocent. He suggested that Smith and the cadet who accused him of rape, had had an on-again, off-again sexual relationship.

The government rested its case late Tuesday morning. The defense was to begin presenting witnesses after a lunch break.

Once the hearing ends, Commander Steven Anderson, who is presiding over the hearing, will prepare a report for the superintendent of the academy, Rear Adm. James C. Van Sice, who must make a final ruling within a week on whether to court-martial Smith.

Smith is working at the Naval Submarine Base in Groton and has been barred from contact with other cadets.

Sexual assaults at the military academies drew national attention in 2004, when nearly 150 women at the Air Force Academy in Colorado came forward with accusations that they had been sexually assaulted by fellow cadets between 1993 and 2003. Many alleged they were ignored or ostracized for speaking out. A Pentagon task force found that hostile attitudes and inappropriate treatment of women also persisted at the U.S. Military Academy at West Point and at the Naval Academy.

The Coast Guard academy, founded in 1876, is the smallest federal service academy with an enrollment of about 980 cadets.

Appendix 15

Convening Authority Decided to Convene General Court-Martial

Coast Guard Cadet to be Court-Martialed

Associated Press | April 13, 2006

NEW HAVEN, Conn. - A cadet at the Coast Guard Academy will face a court-martial on rape and other charges, the first such trial in the institution's history, the school said Wednesday.

Webster M. Smith, 22, faces nine charges including rape, sodomy, extortion and assault.

He had faced misconduct accusations from seven female cadets, ranging from rape to improper touching. Rear Adm. James C. Van Sice, the academy superintendent, dismissed five charges Wednesday, including indecent assault and one sodomy charge.

It was unclear whether any of the accusers were dropped from the case altogether.

The rape charge involves a woman friends described as Smith's on-again, off-again girlfriend, and testimony last month centered on a night of drinking in Annapolis, Md.

One friend testified that the alleged victim passed out and was shocked to learn the next morning that she and Smith had had sex.

The date of the court-martial, the military equivalent of a trial, was not set.

"As we've said from the beginning, Webster Smith is not guilty of these charges, and we will make that demonstration," said defense attorney Merle Smith, no relation to the cadet.

Smith, a senior, remains enrolled but has been barred from contact with other cadets. His status will stay the same until the trial is over, an academy spokesman said. He has not completed the required coursework to be eligible to graduate this spring.

The school is not releasing the identities of the accusers.

The academy, founded in 1876, is the smallest U.S. service academy, with an enrollment of about 980.

Women represent about 30 percent of Coast Guard Academy cadets, compared with less than 20 percent at the Air Force and Naval Academies and about 15 percent at West Point.

www.ingramcontent.com/pod-product-compliance
Lightning Source LLC
Chambersburg PA
CBHW070224190526
45169CB00001B/74